65 billion reasons why you cannot trust Wall Street!

Madoff – 4 years later

A first person journey into the
underworld of Bernard Madoff
by someone who lived it!

Volume I, Revision I

Michael T. De Vita

ISBN:1481141937
ISBN-13:9781481141932

DEDICATION

This book is dedicated to the tens of thousands of investors defrauded by criminals like Bernard Madoff.   Since history tends to repeat itself, this book is also dedicated to you, the future victims of fraud in the U.S. Securities Industry.

Prologue

This book is not just about the past. It is also a book about the future; perhaps YOUR future.

Outright fraud, in a regulated industry! Unthinkable! It just can't happen. Imagine that your investment manager was a fake who simply printed brokerage statements while never executing a single trade. Surely the SEC would IMMEDIATELY detect these activities. After all, the SEC was created to discover crimes just like this and protect investors just like you. But the SEC never discovered the Madoff crime. When the scheme collapsed in 2008 it was because Madoff turned himself in and told authorities that he alone was responsible for the decades long crime.

Now Bernard Madoff is in jail. You might think the Securities Industry is once again safe for investors. You would be wrong!

Why should you care about the Madoff scandal? After all, he was not your investment manager so you lost nothing!

Why should you care about the IMPLICATIONS of the Madoff scandal? Because WHY it happened is still true today – the underlying problems have NOT been fixed. History does tend to repeat itself – especially if nothing changes and the underlying issues are not corrected.

The next time around – it could happen to your investment account.

You are sadly mistaken if you think the Madoff scandal was an aberration. Greed driven excesses leading to criminal activity on Wall Street has happened before. It will happen again. More importantly, you can be absolutely certain that it is happening right now. The newest crimes defrauding Wall Street investors just haven't been discovered yet.

Every investor knows stock prices go down as well as up. What mistakes worry investors most?

- Picking stocks that go down, not up.
- Picking a mutual fund that decreases in value.
- Buying any stock when the whole market is collapsing.
- Selling when you think the bull is dead, but there is still a long run upwards and you fail to participate in that rise.
- Hiring professionals to manage your money where the only "winner" is the paid investment advisor.
- Unexpected news that instantaneously craters the market and your portfolio along with it.

I wager that investment manager fraud was not on your "mistakes" list – it was not on mine.

Bernard L. Madoff was one of the most highly regarded and sought after money managers on Wall Street. He also committed the largest financial crime in history. Madoff duped tens of thousands into believing he was a brilliant investment manager. The scheme ran on for decades, right under the nose of other Wall Street firms, banks, and the Federal Agencies tasked with regulating and policing the securities industry.

At the sentencing hearing on June 29th, 2009 Madoff incredulously told the world he both planned and executed the entire crime himself; no one else was involved. He turned to face the many victims in the courtroom - and tersely apologized. Judge Dennis Chin was unimpressed, sentencing Madoff to the maximum penalty of 150 years. Whilst the 72 year old Madoff will never serve the full sentence, the length is symbolic of the severity and longevity of the crime. Perhaps Judge Chin wanted to send a message to Wall Street that unbridled contempt for innocent investors will be met with unbridled punishment from the justice system. White collar crime is seldom severely punished. A thief may get 10 years for holding up a convenience store and stealing one HUNDRED dollars while a white collar criminal may get 2 years for stealing one hundred MILLION dollars.

In spite of the fact that a number of his relatives worked at the firm, Bernard Madoff and his brother Peter are the only two with the family surname who pleaded guilty to a crime. Bernard is in Butner Federal prison in North Carolina until June 28th, 2159. Peter will be sentenced in August of 2012 and has agreed through a plea bargain to serve at least 10 years.

Peter Madoff pleaded guilty on June 29th, 2012 - exactly 3 years to the day that Bernard was sentenced. But Peter did not plead guilty to knowing his older brother was conducting a fraud. Nor did he admit to materially participating in the Ponzi scheme. Prosecutors accepted a plea arrangement where Peter admitted to conspiracy, falsifying records, filing false tax returns and lying to investigators. Peter agreed to forfeit $143 billion. This symbolic amount represents what prosecutors estimate ran through the criminal enterprise during the decades Peter worked alongside his brother. While Peter Madoff will never be able to pay this enormous sum it is a guarantee that he will enter prison destitute, just like many of those invested in his firm. It is not clear if Madoff's victims will see any of this money or if the Federal Government will keep Peter's assets.

Three and a half years to get Peter - the creaky wheels of justice do turn, they just turn very slowly. Madoff victims continue to hope that someday others who worked with implementing the scandal on a daily basis will also be brought to justice.

The information for this book arises from my own personal experiences along with an exhaustive investigation which included analyzing thousands of pages of complaints filed by the

SIPC Bankruptcy Trustee appointed to liquidate what remains of the Madoff empire, reports from the SEC, discussions with Federal and State legislators and discussions with a number of other Madoff investors and a former Madoff employee.

This book is dedicated to the tens of thousands of investors defrauded by criminals like Bernard Madoff. These investors have been vilified by many who simply do not understand that Madoff was a criminal and his investors are victims of that crime. The victimization did not begin nor does it end with a discussion of Madoff alone. Incompetence by the Federal regulatory agencies allowed Madoff to operate for decades. This negligence did not benefit Madoff's investors, but it did serve to create one massive winner. State and Federal agencies received an enormous tax windfall from the falsified 1099s Madoff churned out.

The press has given extensive coverage to the Madoff crime. But the very nature of the short term focus of the media and the prevalence of the sound bite makes this an inadequate vehicle to tell the entire and rather complex story behind the crime, investors, Wall Street and government.

Madoff is not the first Wall Street guru to cheat his victims. You can be absolutely certain he will not be the last. The Federal agencies tasked with policing the securities industry did not catch Madoff. Only time and failure to attract new investors ended the crime spree. Nothing is really different today – the next Madoff is already running the next scam.

Therefore, this book is also dedicated to YOU, the future victims of fraud in the U.S. Securities Industry.

American investors will benefit by understanding the implications to them of the issues addressed in this book. Because the Madoff crime is complicated – so is this book.

CONTENTS

ACKNOWLEDGMENTS

My mother and I have worked together extensively over the past 4 years to communicate with other Madoff investors, collect information, and prepare the material for this book.   Without her assistance and support this book would not be possible.

1 WHY THIS BOOK?

My Madoff story is being told as a two Volume series. This book, Volume I of the "Madoff chronicles", covers in great detail specifics of how the Madoff crime operated on a day-to-day basis. We will cover how the scheme worked, who was involved, and just how much money was involved.

While the press has given very frequent coverage to the Madoff event it has failed to provide the detail you will see in this book. It simply is not possible for the press to provide this degree of information – it is too complex for a short news segment or even a lengthy documentary.

Volume I ends with the a description of the "typical Madoff investor" and recounts a powerful exchange between Congressman Ackerman and SEC officials during a hearing in Washington, D.C. The story of "follow the money" as it relates to Madoff family members was intended to appear in Volume II, but this chapter was added to this book based on the sentencing hearing event of Peter Madoff on December 20, 2012.

Volume II tells you how the victims mobilized into interest groups and discusses the role of governmental agencies like the SEC and Congress as well as the activities of congressionally authorized agencies tasked with compensating investors when a Wall Street brokerage fails.

A highly respected Wall Street investment manager turns out to be a thief. $65 billion dollars is missing. There are tens of thousands of victims. This collapse of this crime coincided with the 2008 financial crisis which nearly led to the next Great Depression. Financial firms, Wall Street brokerages, banks, private mortgage lenders and even quasi-governmental mortgage lenders were all taking huge financial risks and dragging the U.S. economy into the abyss.

Bernie Madoff's arrest was completely unexpected. The media frenetically assigned personnel tasked with investigating the biggest financial crime in the history of the planet. Ground-breaking coverage of this scandal could be a career builder. The Madoff story could be the nation's financial Watergate. A reporter in the right place, asking the right questions of the right people could be the next Woodward or Bernstein. Could there be another "deep throat" out there willing to give some reporter the inside track on the largest financial crime in the history of the planet?

Was this a real crime or was it just a Wall Street maven with a short term problem caused by the nation's financial crisis?

Immediately after Madoff's arrest, his attorney, Daniel Horwitz, suggested that no crime was committed. Horwitz told the media *"Bernie Madoff is a long-standing leader in the financial services industry. He will fight to get through this unfortunate set of events."* Horwitz was wrong! Within days it became very clear that this was not just "an unfortunate situation," it was a financial and emotional catastrophe for those invested with

BLMIS (Bernard L. Madoff Investment Securities).

News organizations reported Madoff told investors they were worth $64.5 billion. In reality, most of that existed only on paper. There was a near total absence of reliable information as to how much was left. The bee hive of news media swarmed around every piece of data, no matter how small. For those investors willing to talk to the press, the phone rang incessantly with calls from reporters asking for comments about the news item of the moment. How do you comment about something when you know almost nothing? How do you characterize an investment advisor most never met, never talked to, and never considered anything more than the name on the monthly statements received from the brokerage house which managed their future, their retirement and controlled their financial security.

I was one of those investors.

During the next few months I spent a great deal of time asking myself these questions.

> How do you steal $65 billion? Is it really possible that Bernie Madoff carried out this fraud all by himself? Who else might be involved? Where were the Federal watchdogs and why didn't the SEC discover this fraud much earlier while it was still small? Did Wall Street know what Madoff was doing? Did the financial wizards on Wall Street profit from Madoff and therefore choose to ignore whatever it was he was doing? Who else invested with Madoff? Can we help each other? Did Bernie steal all the money for himself or did others benefit from the crime? How much is left and how long will it take to get those assets back to investors? Can Federal or

State legislators help?

The Madoff sentencing on June 29th, 2009 was covered by domestic and international news outlets. The story had drawn worldwide attention for many reasons, including the sheer amount of money involved and the many thousands of victimized investors (one source estimates that nearly 300,000 people may have been affected by this fraud worldwide). Since Madoff's arrest in December of 2008, governmental and private sector organizations were all investigating the crime and news stories appeared on financial networks and in the mainstream media just about every single day.

I read everything I could find and began to assemble a data base that would hopefully help answer my growing list of questions. Several hundred Madoff investors banded together to share information on an internet forum. In the early days, this forum was truly a "band of brothers"; we were all in the same boat, and the boat was sinking. A typical day would have over 100 emails submitted by investors. This "information sharing" allowed me to get a perspective on what other investors were thinking and provided access to what was being reported by the media throughout the nation.

Six more months passed attempting to catalogue and digest all this data. Under the direction of one imaginative Madoff investor named Alexandra Roth, 29 Madoff investors told their personal stories of how each came to invest with BLMIS and how their lives changed as a result of the crime that made those investments totally worthless. This attempt to combat the stereotype of the wealthy Madoff investor became a book titled "The Club No One Wanted to Join." This book included stories by victims from across the spectrum – small investors, large investors, retirees, young people, professionals, blue collar workers, direct investors, and those who invested through one of the many funds that gave their client's money to Madoff to invest (feeder funds).

A local college offers adult education classes on a variety of topics. One class is titled "Meet the Author." Since I was one of the 29 authors of "The Club No One Wanted to Join" I contacted the instructor and offered to be a guest speaker at the class. I was well aware of the misinformation in "the cloud" and the investor stereotype being put forth by the media. I hoped to dispel at least some of these myths by talking at this 90 minute long class. Typically the speaker would present material about the book for one hour and then take questions for 30 minutes. It was actually quite easy to prepare a 60 minute presentation. By this point I had a substantial amount of data collected over many months, and I had my personal story in the book to talk about. The immense degree of detailed data collected combined with excerpts from the personal stories of others participating in the book would make a very engaging and entertaining discussion for the class. On Tuesday, November 2nd, 2010 I gave the lecture at the college. It was extremely well received and lasted close to 2 hours. The instructor asked if I would be interested in developing an entire course on the Madoff Fraud for the next semester.

Creating material for an entire semester would prove to be an order of magnitude more difficult than a single class as a guest speaker. On Monday, November 15th, 2010 I met the person who organizes the program at a local Starbucks to discuss the possibility of teaching a course about the Madoff saga for the next semester starting in February of 2011. It was then that I discovered I would be expected to teach a 12 week course with each lecture lasting 90 minutes.

It was one thing to produce a 60 minute talk built around a previously published book. It was quite another to produce 18 hours of lectures.

I had eleven weeks from this initial meeting on November 15th, 2010 until the first class on February 8th, 2011.

Thus began a concerted effort to consolidate information gathered over the past 2 years and organize it into a cogent and persuasive documentary on the Madoff scandal and its effect on not only Madoff investors but also on the entire American investor population. For me, success meant not only educating the class to understand the specifics of Madoff's crime, but also helping the audience recognize flaws in our investor protection system. Students had to understand how failures by Wall Street and Federal regulators cause enormous damage to those who place their trust and their financial future in the hands of the securities industry which is overseen and regulated by our government.

For years our government and financial planners have been imploring Americans to save for retirement. For years, our politicians tell us "if you work hard and play by the rules then you will get ahead." Madoff's crime is a glaring example of what happens when you follow those directives - and the system betrays you.

The Bankruptcy Trustee appointed by the Securities Investment Protection Corporation (SIPC) to liquidate BLMIS (Bernard L. Madoff Investment Securities) and accumulate assets for later distribution to investors became an unanticipated source of information presented in my lectures and in this book. This trustee filed hundreds of lawsuits against a variety of individuals and organizations. Many of these lawsuits were against "small" investors - the very investors that the securities law was intended to protect -- and organizations, both large and small, including pension plans and charitable organizations. The more important lawsuits for me were against those the trustee considered complicit in the Ponzi scheme.

The effort to prepare the lectures led me to be one of the very few to actually review several thousand pages of litigation from this data rich source. Although many of the claims made in this litigation are allegations only (a trial or confession would be needed to make them facts), those claims do tell a compelling story of how Madoff executed the crime and provides detailed information of the role played by others whom I choose to describe as Madoff's accomplices.

Another major source of information for this book came from a report published by the Office of Investigations of the U.S. Securities and Exchange Commission (SEC) on August 31, 2009. This report is titled "Investigation of Failure of the SEC to Uncover Bernard Madoff's Ponzi Scheme – Public Version." Considering the damaging comments about the competence of the agency tasked with policing the securities industry, one can only wonder what is in the non-public version. This extensive 477 page report proved invaluable in writing the lectures on how our government not only failed to discover the crime but actually allowed the scheme to flourish for decades as Madoff promoted to his clients that he successfully passed multiple SEC examinations. Madoff, the master con man, used this imprimatur of approval by a federal agency to encourage others to feel confident investing with him. The specifics of multiple failed investigations of BLMIS provides an insight into why the SEC needs to be reformed to better protect American investors.

No new laws were needed to discover the Madoff scheme. The SEC simply needed to enforce laws already in place and conduct just a single competent examination of his trading activity. Indeed, the SEC had all the laws, powers and information needed to end this crime in 1992.

One additional source contributed significantly to the course and this book – Congress. The SEC is tasked with regulating the industry and periodically investigating registered and licensed broker dealers. In the Madoff case, the SEC failed miserably. Multiple Congressional hearings in D.C. (many of which I attended) where witnesses testified under oath provided information to better understand not only how the regulatory agencies failed so miserably to discover Madoff, but also suggested options where Congress could help to compensate crime victims and attempt to reverse some of the damage done by Madoff right under the nose of the agency that was supposed to stop this from happening.

Congress has an obligation not only to current financial crime victims, but also to future victims. Legislation can limit the ability of others to commit similar crimes by properly funding and managing the SEC, and by making Wall Street financially responsible for damages done by one of their own. The second book in this series details how Congress performed in the Madoff case. That performance raises serious questions about whether legislation to actually fix the problems identified by the Madoff crime will ever be passed.

Over the past 2 years I invested more than 400 hours collecting, organizing and analyzing data. I started to write lectures for the class in early December of 2010. Eight weeks later only four lectures were finished. Since the first class started in one short week, additional lectures would be written concurrent with giving a lecture. By the end of March nine of the twelve lectures were complete. But there was now a new problem. Half the notes yielded lectures for three-fourths of the semester. There was too much material to fit into 18 hours of lectures. In addition I was overly optimistic about how much could be covered in each 90 minute class. I did not consider the number or complexity of questions posed by attendees. These insightful questions were used to modify lectures for future classes by proactively addressing issues identified by current students. Since the semester could not be extended, I removed some material from the lectures and asked very willing attendees to lengthen each class by 15 minutes.

With the class I now had an opportunity to entertain, educate and inform others about the holes in the leaky protection system currently in place. But I was only educating about 20 persons at a time. Thus one more reason for this book – it is an opportunity to significantly broaden the base and tell this classroom tested story to many more people.

On Tuesday, May 8, 2012 I joined with a number of other Madoff investors in New York for a demonstration focusing on "The Death of the American Investor." The purpose was to gain support for a house bill (HR 757) that would guarantee the statement an investor receives from a licensed broker-dealer carries legal weight. Madoff investors found their statements were deemed worthless by the trustee. This bill, which protects investors by forcing Wall Street to honor statements printed by its members – is going nowhere.

At this demonstration I met Eleanar Squillari who introduced herself as Bernard Madoff's longtime private secretary. Eleanor told me she has been cooperating with authorities for some time and was now working with a film crew to produce a documentary on the Madoff scandal. Unlike most of his investors, she knew all of the Madoffs personally. A lively conversation ensued for the next 30 minutes and Eleanor and I found we had a very different perspective of the involvement of Madoff family members. Eleanor's view was colored by her personal experience with these individuals; mine was formed by evaluating the information you will read in this book.

A few days after the NY demonstration the producer called and asked if I could attend an interview at Columbia University in NY; this was to be one of the final "shoots" for the documentary. It was not possible to go to NY on one day's notice. I thought that was the end of that and I looked forward to seeing the documentary with the tentative title of "In God We Trust."

The next week another call from the producer ensued asking if they could come to my location for a "short filming" that would add about one minute to the documentary. The crew arrived about 11 a.m. on June 26th. The caravan included four cars, several cameras and six people. The "short filming" lasted 7 hours. Over the course of the past 3 ½ years I interacted frequently with the press appearing in a number of TV interviews and was often quoted in many, many newspaper and magazine articles. This was my first experience with "reshoots" where the stripped bar appears and you hear words like "scene two, take three." The experience showed how difficult it is to actually produce a film. It was quite fascinating and informative.

After the work part of day was over I had a lengthy chat with the producer and together we reviewed a number of the lectures I prepared for the course. She asked me why I had not converted this information into a book. I did not have a good answer.

This book is not going to retroactively change the law as it existed in 2008 when Madoff confessed. Therefore, it is not going to help Madoff investors; it is too late for them! My real hope is that it will change my fellow American's perception of the average Madoff investor and that it will cause a groundswell of support for changes to the laws that ostensibly protect brokerage customers.

So "why this book"? The American investor public has a right to know what really happened and how decisions impacting Madoff investors have set precedents that will affect future investors. The class has been very well received and the significant effort put forth to write these lectures deserves to be extended to those unable to attend the class. If this book helps even a single investor to avoid the trauma of involvement in a Madoff like scandal then the additional effort to convert the class into a book will be justified.

Finally, it is a great mental health exercise for me!

2 WING-IT INVESTMENT SECURITIES

Perhaps the best way to describe the "Madoff experience" is with a fictional example. For the purposes of this book, the name of the investment company is "Wing-It Investment Securities."

This chart was taken from the very first lecture of my class and served as the basis for a discussion tracing a single investor through the process of attending an investment seminar, accepting the pitch, watching the investment grow, retiring with assets accumulated in the account, and suffering the fallout of the failure of the firm due to the criminal activity of the principle.

Wing-It Investment Securities

Experience
Integrity
Safety
Diversification
Capital preservation
Proprietary trading system
Long-term track record

**Investment Professionals
Since 1960**

We treat your money like it is our own

☐ The year is 1990
☐ You receive an offer to attend a seminar about investing for retirement and decide to attend

15

Let's set the stage. The year is 1990. You are 50 years old and have hit the peak of your earning potential. You have always been a saver and now your thoughts turn seriously toward retirement. It is only 15 years away. You receive a letter in the mail inviting you to a local investment seminar that focuses on long term retirement planning and investing for the future. You reply to the offer and attend the seminar.

The speaker is the CEO of Wing-It Investment Securities who proves to be a very dynamic and convincing presenter. But it is not just his words that impact you; it is his resume and the track record for the firm's investment advisory business.

Here is what you learn about Wing-It during the course of the seminar.

- The firm
    - Wing-It has been in business since 1959
    - The firm has over 400 employees
    - It is one of the largest market makers on Wall Street with $1 trillion a year in trading volume
    - Member of the Securities Investor Protection Corporation (SIPC). Your account is insured for up to $500,000
    - Member of the Financial Industry Regulator Authority (FINRA), the largest independent regulator for all securities firms doing business in the United States
    - Carries additional insurance through Lloyds of London for $10,000,000 per account
    - Authorized by the IRS to handle IRA and pension accounts
    - Like all investment firms, Wing-It is investigated by the SEC every few years and has successfully passed 6 SEC examinations

- The CEO
    - The owner of the company is well known and respected on Wall Street
    - Considered an innovator by his peers
    - Conceived and helped develop computerized trading software which eventually led to the creation of the National Association of Securities Dealers Automated Quotations (NASDAQ)
    - Two-time Chairman of the Board of Directors of the NASDAQ

- On the Board of Governors of the National Association of Securities Dealers (NASD)
- On the Board of Directors of the Securities Industry Association
- Frequent consultant to the SEC

- The Investment Advisory service of Wing-It
  - Uses a modification of the trading software that led to the creation of NASDAQ to develop a proprietary trading process called a "Split Strike Conversion Strategy"
  - This proprietary software is used for all customer investment accounts
  - This improved software is ideally suited to long term planning
  - The objective and promise of this strategy is to smooth out investment returns.   It will not give investors the highest returns in any given year, but it will produce consistent results in both good and bad markets
  - Historical reports demonstrate that this strategy does limit the upside gain for an account thus capping annual growth - but more importantly it also limits the downside risk in bad markets making it ideal for retirement planning
  - In order to ensure stability and liquidity Wing-It trades ONLY fortune 500 companies; no trading in higher risk investments involving IPOs or penny stocks
  - The Wing-It strategy has been used successfully since the mid 1960s and has generated returns of 8-12% a year

- Many of the rich and famous are clients of Wing-It
- Wing-It offers two investment programs. With a minimum deposit of $100,000 you can open an individual managed brokerage account. Smaller deposits will be pooled with other investors who will buy shares in the Wing-It Income Fund

The presentation is fascinating. The charts shown during the presentation indicate a battle tested strategy that is ideally suited for a stable, low volatility, long term retirement program.

You, along with a number of other seminar participants, decide to open an account. Within a few days you deposit the minimum startup value of $100,000 into a managed Wing-It individual brokerage account.

The year is now 2001. You are 60 years old and your net worth has increased substantially over the past decade. All of your investments have done well. The S&P 500 Index returned an average of 19% annually over the past decade and your investments with large mutual fund companies have performed in line with the overall market.

Wing-It has not done as well as the S&P, but, as promised during the seminar 10 years ago, it has been much more consistent. The S&P 500 had very wide year-to-year fluctuations. The index returned MINUS 3.2% in 1990 and POSITIVE 37.4% in 1995. By contrast, the Wing-It account returned not less than 8% in any year and not more than 12%. The average return for the account was 10%; respectable, but far below the long term S&P average. As promised by the Wing-It CEO, the Wing-It account returned stable, consistent returns useful for long-term planning.

Now let's look at your situation in early January of 2001.

- Wing-It produced monthly statements and confirmations showing buys and sells of Fortune 500 companies along with annual reports from an accounting firm that audits Wing-It's books
- The account returned between 8% and 12% during the past 10 years; averaging 10%
- Your original investment of $100,000 is now worth $250,000
- You received 1099s each year and paid $50,000 in Federal taxes and $5,000 in State income taxes on the $150,000 in reported gains
- You speak with Wing-It's actuary who tells you this account will last more than 10 years if you take out $40,000 each year

Given your personal financial situation you decide to retire at 60 and begin collecting annual checks from your Wing-It account. The first check for $40,000 arrives in mid-January of 2001.

Your new life style includes buying a house in Florida and becoming a snowbird by wintering in the warm weather of the Gulf State. Your golf handicap drops by 10 strokes and you make many new friends. You tell many in your new social circle about your Wing-It experience. Some of your new friends decide to open an account.

Fast forward eight years to January of 2009. You have made annual $40,000 withdrawals from your Wing-It account. The remaining balance continues to earn an average 10% annual return. Of course, you continue to pay taxes on those gains as reported on the 1099s you receive each year; paying an additional $44,592 in Federal tax and $4,500 in State Income tax. The following table shows the end of year balances in your Wing-It brokerage account.

By 2008, you have withdrawn a total of $320,000 and your account is still worth $107,692.

Year	Account Value	Gains (10% annually)	With-drawals
2001	$250,000	$25,000	$40,000
2002	$235,000	$23,500	$40,000
2003	$218,500	$21,850	$40,000
2004	$200,350	$20,035	$40,000
2005	$180,385	$18,039	$40,000
2006	$158,424	$15,842	$40,000
2007	$134.266	$13,427	$40,000
2008	**$107,692**	$10,769	$40,000
Totals		$148,642	**$320,000**

The plan is working. Life is good!

It is now January of 2009.

- You hear a news flash on January 1, 2009 that Wing-Its' owner has been arrested for running a decades long Ponzi scheme
- You have been receiving trade confirmations and monthly brokerage statements for over 20 years. You know that Wing-It passed six SEC examinations and you believe that the SEC must have verified Wing-It's trading activity. Your account must be safe
- You tell yourself that the Wing-It Income mutual fund is the center of the fraud and "the other guys" that put their money in the fund are wiped out
- It is likely that your check for $40,000 will not be "in the mail"
- But, all is not lost
    - Wing-It carried SIPC insurance, just like every other SEC licensed broker-dealer
    - You KNOW that your brokerage account is SIPC insured for up to $500,000
    - Just like FDIC coverage at your bank, you believe that you will shortly get back the $107,692 value of your account that showed on your last statement dated December 31, 2008
    - As a fail-safe, Wing-It also carried additional insurance through Lloyds of London

Wing-It investors are being vilified in the press. The American population in general has accepted the media stereotype of greedy, selfish, arrogant investors who took these incredible returns and got what they deserved. The concept that Wing-It investors are no different from other Main Street investors who make well-considered long term investment decisions is totally discounted. Wing-It investors are treated by the press as virtual criminals.

It is now April of 2009 and the consequences of the brokerage failure are now quite clear to you.

- SIPC assigns a trustee to dispose of Wing-Its' assets
- The trustee says that since you put in $100,000 and took out $320,000 over the years you are classified as a "net-winner", i.e. you took out more than your original investment
- The trustee has chosen to completely ignore all of the statements you received from Wing-It over the past 2 decades and only approve SIPC coverage for the net equity of each account
- Since you put in $100,000 and took out $320,000 you have a net equity of MINUS $220,000
- Your application for SIPC coverage of your last account balance of $107,692 has been denied and SIPC will pay you nothing
- The Lloyds of London supplemental insurance policy was as fictional as your brokerage statements
- You discover that the trustee expects to recover several billion dollars from the Wing-It liquidation and believe that you will eventually get some portion of that recovery.
- Then you learn that the trustee will not be making any distributions of recovered funds to "net winners" – you will get nothing of the $107,692 shown in your final statement
    - But it gets worse - you are being sued by the trustee for $220,000; every penny that you took

out over the past six years that exceeded your original investment

■ You hire an attorney to defend the claims of the trustee and an accountant to attempt to file amended tax returns

■ The taxing agencies consider the 1099s valid while the SIPC trustee considers the statements showing this identical income invalid

■ You contact your member of the US House of Representatives to seek assistance in recovering taxes paid on the 1099s for income that never existed. Only a few Wing-It investors live in the congressman's district and there is no public pressure to address the morality of the IRS's windfall profit on the nonexistent income. Your phone calls and emails are not returned

■ You find that you may still owe State income tax on the 1099 "earned" income for the first 11 months of 2008 before Wing-It collapsed

■ Your income has dropped dramatically from $4,733 a month to your Social Security check of $1,400 a month.

■ With your reduced income and new expenses for legal and accounting services you cannot pay the mortgage on your home

■ You sell your Florida home (for less than the mortgage amount, after all, in 2009 the real estate bubble is alive and well and home prices are collapsing)

■ You try to find a job and discover that few want to hire a 68 year old who has been out of the workforce for 8 years

■ You move in with your adult children who just love the idea of having grandpop available to serve as the day care provider for the grandchildren

You have just experienced SOME of the issues and difficulties faced by Bernard L. Madoff investors.

Replace the name "Wing-It Investment Securities" with "Bernard Madoff Investment Securities" and you will learn that this book has real meaning for you.

3 THE BEGINNING

In 1990 I was working for a small firm with an office in the University City Science Center in Philadelphia. Now in my late thirties I was in the midst of the highest earning period of my career. I maximized those earnings by working as many hours as I could. A six day work week was not out of the ordinary.

My conservative family upbringing taught me that saving part of what you earn is a central element of a successful lifetime financial plan. I found that I was earning significantly more than I was spending and needed a place to invest the surplus. The primary goal was to find an investment vehicle suited to implementing a long-term retirement plan which would factor in a relatively consistent rate of return with low volatility.

The University City Science Center, located near the University of Pennsylvania and Drexel University, presented a resource for small companies to operate in a synergistic and supportive environment to develop new ideas and evaluate the marketability of innovative products and business concepts. The Center had a co-ed softball league where employees of many different companies (most were small and could not field an entire team) got together to play a friendly game of softball once a week during late Spring and Summer. One day during a game the discussion turned to how, and where, to invest. One person, I think it was our centerfielder, suggested a firm he had been using to manage his money for the past few years. That firm was Avellino and Bienes (A&B), an accounting firm run by Frank Avellino and Michael Bienes. During the course of the next few days I contacted the firm and, after carefully inspecting the firm's track record, opened two investment accounts. One was in my name, and the other was a joint account for my parents. This was the first time that anyone in the family hired a professional money manager. Unfortunately, it was not to be the last.

A&B portrayed itself as a professional investment firm engaging in something they called "convertible arbitrage." In simple terms, the arbitrage system employed by A&B means that the firm buys an investment selling at a discount in one country and then immediately sells it in another country for a slightly higher price. The firm claimed a track record that showed years of steady returns. If memory serves me correctly, I believe that A&B's historical material showed about a 12% annual return. As the chart below shows, that return would actually be BELOW the S&P 500 for the 1990 to 1999 period. The rate of return was not the reason to invest with this firm; the low volatility was. Accepting a very consistent but below market return allowed an investor to sleep well at night knowing there would not be a year with significant losses that could decimate a portfolio. This was a great place for a conservative investor unwilling to accept great risk.

This chart shows annual market returns for 30 years. The average return for each ten year segment is 24%, 19% and 12% - all at or well above the historical return for the A&B account. However, note the great volatility in any 10 year period – this volatility was absent from the A&B record.

Historical S&P 500 Index Stock Market Returns					
Year	Return	Year	Return	Year	Return
1980	32.40%	1990	-3.20%	2000	-9.10%
1981	-4.90%	1991	30.50%	2001	-11.90%
1982	21.40%	1992	7.70%	2002	-22.10%
1983	22.5	1993	10.00%	2003	28.70%
1984	6.30%	1994	1.30%	2004	10.90%
1985	32.20%	1995	37.40%	2005	4.90%
1986	18.50%	1996	23.10%	2006	15.90%
1987	5.20%	1997	33.40%	2007	5.50%
1988	16.80%	1998	28.60%	2008	-37.00%
1989	31.50%	1999	21.00%	2009	26.50%
Avg	24.1%		19.0%		12.3%

My understanding at the time was that A&B engaged in taking positions in the currencies of a number of different countries and profiting by taking advantage of fluctuations in the value of these currencies. For a novice investor like myself, this was really "black magic" and I have to admit, I really did not know how A&B executed this strategy. No supporting documentation or investment transactions were reported on the A&B statements;

just the beginning and ending account balances. After about 2 years of receiving these monthly statements my parents and I decided that we should close the accounts and move to a more transparent investment vehicle similar to that offered by mutual funds like Vanguard. We never got the chance to close the account.

In 1992 the SEC conducted an investigation of A&B following allegations that the firm might be running a Ponzi scheme. A&B was charged with "selling securities in unregistered transactions to investors in violation of the law." An SEC investigation led to the closure of A&B and a receiver was appointed by the court to return A&B assets to investors. The SEC enforcement action discovered that almost all of the A&B funds were actually invested with BLMIS (Bernard L Madoff Investment Securities). According to the SEC, A&B was not investing in currency arbitrage. In fact, the firm was not investing at all. Investor money was simply being given to BLMIS.

Still an investing novice, I did not really understand the specifics of what this meant to A&B investors. I did know that the money in the account was at risk and that A&B was not really a money management firm. In fact, A&B was nothing more than a front for this firm called BLMIS. With a great sense of relief I read an article published in the Wall Street Journal in 1992 reporting the results of the SEC investigation of A&B. This WSJ article indicated that A&B was serving only as a feeder fund for BLMIS and the SEC found that all investor money was actually being held and managed by BLMIS. Indeed, the article went on to quote Martin Kuperberg, the SEC Associate Regional Administrator in New York who said:

"there was no indication of fraud" at the "real" money manager. None of the officials involved in the case would disclose the name of the broker-dealer whose trading apparently produced results good enough to draw in such a large sum of money. However, Mr. Kuperberg said that the returns appeared to have been generated legitimately "Right now, there's nothing to indicate fraud," he said.

The press reported that the manager was Bernard Madoff, head of Bernard L. Madoff Investment Securities (BLMIS). Madoff was described as one of the most highly respected money managers on Wall Street. Years later, specific details remain fuzzy, but I do believe a letter from BLMIS stated that, although my account was small, since I was already an investor at the firm through A&B, I could simply open a direct account with BLMIS with the proceeds of the A&B liquidation.

Like most Madoff investors, I had never heard of Bernard Madoff nor did I ever meet or speak with him. The name of the firm and the name on the statements read BLMIS. From my perspective, BLMIS, which contained the name of its founder, could easily have had a different name like Merrill Lynch which also was named after principals and founders of the firm.

SEC *Breaks Up Investment Company That Paid Off Big but Didn't Register*

BY RANDALL SMITH

Staff Reporter of THE WALL STREET JOURNAL [12/1/92]

Two Florida accountants have returned $441 million to investors after regulators charged them with a huge sale of unregistered securities, their lawyer said.

The two accountants, Frank J. Avellino and Michael S. Bienes of Fort Lauderdale, promised, and apparently delivered, annual returns of 13.5% to 20% to their investors. Their main office is located in New York City.

However, in a complaint filed Nov. 17 in federal Court in Manhattan, the Securities and Exchange Commission charged the two men with operating an unregistered investment company because they didn't register as securities the promissory notes they gave their investors.

Investments in Stocks

The SEC complaint said the money collected from investors was turned over to an unnamed broker-dealer, who managed the accounts at his own discretion. One person familiar with the case said the broker put the money into listed stocks. The complaint said Messrs. Avellino and Bienes kept the difference between the fixed interest they paid to investors and the returns generated by the broker's investment decisions.

In an announcement, the law firm for the two accountants, Squadron, Ellenoff, Plesent & Lehrer, said the partnership of Avellino & Bienes is dissolving and had returned all principal and interest due its noteholders as of Nov. 16. Ira Lee Sorkin, a partner in the law firm, said the return was completed Nov. 24.

The SEC said the two men ended their 22-year-old accounting practice and began focusing exclusively on their more-profitable investing business in 1984.

Although 13.5% to 20% rates of return are high by historical standards, they wouldn't have been impossible to attain. For example, from Jan. 1, 1984, to Oct. 31, 1992, the Vanguard Group stock index fund showed a 14.85% annual return, according to Morningstar Inc., a mutual fund data service.

As of Oct. 30, the SEC said the two men had nine different trading accounts with the broker-dealer with an equity value of $454 million. At the same time, they had issued notes totaling $441 million either through new sales to investors or the rollover of interest payments.

Martin Kuperberg, SEC senior associate regional administrator in New York, said, "The investing public must get the protection afforded by the federal securities laws, such as a prospectus, certified reports, and fidelity bonds." However, Mr. Sorkin said his clients didn't know they were subject to such requirements.

'Nothing to Indicate Fraud'

None of the officials involved in the case would disclose the name of the broker-dealer whose trading apparently produced results good enough to draw in such a large sum of money. However, Mr. Kuperberg said that the returns appeared to have been generated legitimately "Right now, there's nothing to indicate fraud," he said.

Neither Mr. Avellino nor Mr. Bienes, both 56 years old, were available to comment, according to their New York office. Mr. Sorkin characterized the sales of unregistered securities as "technical violations."

The investors' money was ordered returned by federal judge Kenneth Conboy, who named New York attorney Lee Richards as trustee. Mr. Richards, in turn, has hired the accounting firm of Price Waterhouse & Co. to audit the partnership's financial records.

Slide from class of Wall Street Journal article – 12/1/1992

I have since found that many former A&B investors were likewise offered accounts with BLMIS. The key question for me and all other A&B investors was "who is Bernard Madoff and can he be trusted with my money?"

The article in the Wall Street Journal on December 1st, 1992 helped to address this question.

What did I learn from the WSJ article?

1. The money, including gains, was all there.
2. The SEC senior regional manager reported that "there's nothing to indicate fraud" so the possibility of some kind of criminal scheme was erased.
3. The returns were legitimate and the "brains" behind the investments was attributed to an "unnamed broker-dealer" in NY. This turned out to be Bernard Madoff, president of BLMIS.
4. The money was invested in stocks, not the currency arbitrage approach that I previously feared.
5. A&B basically did nothing but recruit new investors for BLMIS making money by keeping part of the reported gains on each account.

Follow up information indicated that BLMIS was a highly respected broker-dealer and Bernard Madoff had a reputation as a sought after money manager. Armed with this information and the near endorsement of Madoff by the SEC, both my parents and I deposited the A&B checks into new accounts at BLMIS. A review of the first BLMIS statement addressed THE major problem with A&B which reported only starting and ending account values. The BLMIS statements showed detailed transactions involving Fortune 500 stocks and U.S. Treasury bills. The sense of relief was immense and immediate. My new money manager was trading REAL stocks with real names that I could track in the financial news. Take a look at the following Madoff monthly statement and note that he reported trading

well known, highly visible securities listed on the major
exchanges as well as U.S. Treasury Bills.

Madoff promoted his investment approach and results as a reason to invest with the firm. The promise, market returns without market volatility, was very appealing. The myth often espoused by the press is that Madoff provided unbelievably high returns. A comparison of returns received by most Madoff investors versus long term results posted by large mutual fund companies yields a very different conclusion. It was not high returns that led many to the Madoff slaughter house, it was low volatility. Remember the chart showing S&P returns over the past 3 decades – well Madoff account holders underperformed those returns.

Although Madoff treated specifics of his approach as a proprietary trade secret, it was generally described as a "split strike conversion strategy." This strategy incorporated stock transactions with a form of hedging to protect against vacillations in the market.

As every investor knows, stocks go up and stocks go down. The key to making a profit is to buy low and sell high; easy to say, difficult to do. The hedging strategy addresses the issue of stock volatility by using S&P Options as a form of volatility insurance on the stock trades. A very simple explanation of the rational for hedging using Options is to smooth out investment returns by reducing the effect of declines in stock prices. For example, if stocks decrease in value then the Option would protect you from much of the decline thus limiting losses. If the stocks purchased go up in value then the Option insurance would never be used and the account would recover nothing for the amount paid for this insurance thus offsetting the increase in stock value and setting a ceiling on profits. This is akin to buying auto insurance. If you have an accident then the insurance covers most of the cost of the accident (less a deductible). If you do not have any accidents then the insurance essentially expires worthless and would have to be renewed to continue insuring the auto. For

BLMIS, using Options would limit both upside gains (because the cost of Options as an insurance would be lost) as well as limiting downside losses (because the cost of Options as an insurance would be used to reduce losses due to declines in stock prices).

The Madoff style was to execute transactions involving a basket of about 60 stocks and supporting Options several times a year. Every customer account would be "all-in" with that account's proportional share of the security basket or "all-out" when proceeds would be used to purchase short term U.S. Treasury bills. The timing of this round trip rotation would be determined by the market guru - Bernard Madoff.

Madoff was NOT a stock picker, he was a market timer. The basket of stocks in the "all-in" strategy was always the same (there were slight variations in the mix over time). Returns were based on the money manager's skill in timing when to buy and when to sell the basket. This Midas-touch of market timing is what supposedly made Madoff a cut above other investment advisors

4 TWO BUSINESSES, ONE LEGITIMATE AND ONE A CRIMINAL ENTERPRISE

Exactly who was Bernard Madoff and how did he become the founder of a firm that would eventually steal $65 billion from his customers and land him in jail for 150 years.

In order to understand Madoff's actions you have to consider his possible motivation. Bernard Madoff was not born into a wealthy family.   But he did have lofty ideas. He was ambitious and he had a persuasive personality that led others to trust and believe in him.   The yardstick for success on Wall Street is measured in money.   Madoff wanted the respect of others in the securities industry, and, as events demonstrate, he was willing to do almost anything to make a lot of money and gain that respect.

Wikipedia.org reported background information not only on Bernard Madoff but also his parents. This information helps to set the stage for the early days as his parents were forced by regulators to leave the Securities industry about the time their son Bernard entered that same industry.

Bernard Madoff was the son of Ralph and Sylvia Madoff.   Ralph began his career as a plumber and eventually decided on the more lucrative occupation of a stockbroker. Sylvia Madoff registered Gibraltar Securities as a broker-dealer. Gibraltar Securities had no formal offices. It was not located near the hub of Wall Street activity. Rather, the corporate office of Gibraltar Securities was registered at the family home in the Laurelton neighborhood of Queens, N.Y. It is difficult to understand why a brokerage business would be located in a personal home. Such a location would not create the appropriate image of a successful broker-dealer when meeting new clients.

It is also difficult to understand why the business would be registered in Sylvia's name. If you consider the time frame of the late 1950's many women did not work outside the home, and few worked on Wall Street. One possible reason for registering Gibraltar Securities in his wife's name is because Ralph Madoff had a federal income tax lien assessed in 1956 in the amount of $13,245.28 (in 2010 this would be more than $100,000). This tax was not paid until 1965, after the SEC forced the closure of Gibraltar Securities.

There is no detailed information available about this firm, no client list, and no information as to any of the firms trading activity. There is also no reported evidence that Bernard Madoff ever worked at this firm.

Like their son and BLMIS almost five decades later, Gibraltar Securities violated securities industry regulations. In August of 1963 the SEC announced it was "instituting proceedings...to determine whether" 48 broker-dealers, including "Sylvia R. Madoff [DBA (doing business as)] Gibraltar Securities," had "failed to file reports of their financial condition...and if so, whether their registrations should be revoked."

In January 1964 the investigation abruptly terminated as the SEC dismissed administrative proceedings against Gibraltar Securities and several other firms. Apparently the SEC and these broker-dealer firms made a deal: if the individuals agree to never again work in the securities industry there would be no penalties and no further prosecution.

"The firms conceded the violation," the SEC noted, "but requested withdrawal of their registrations; and in this connection they represented that they are no longer engaged in the securities business and do not owe any cash or securities to customers. The Commission concluded that the public interest would be served by permitting withdrawal, and discontinued its proceedings."

The Madoff family, Ralph, Sylvia and Bernard all had difficulties following regulations associated with being an SEC licensed broker dealer. Perhaps Bernard did learn something from his parents about how to evade securities laws. If so, his actions over the next 40 years demonstrated that he was much better at it than his parents.

Bernard did have two siblings. Peter, his brother, came to work at BLMIS in 1965. Like his brother with the Madoff surname, Peter pleaded guilty to violations of securities laws on June 29th, 2012.

Let's take a moment and profile Bernard Madoff's early years.

Bernard Madoff was born is 1938. He was a member of his high school swim team and worked summers as a lifeguard. Bernard Madoff showed his entrepreneurial spirit by starting a small business installing lawn sprinklers. Bernard went on to earn a bachelor's degree in political science (likely forging valuable skills for dealing with politicians over the next five decades), and continued his education by completing one year of law school. In 1959 he met and married Ruth Alpern.

Michael T. De Vita

The legitimate business

The lawn sprinkler business was just the beginning for the entrepreneur Bernard Madoff. In 1959 Bernard followed in the footsteps of his parents and founded his own broker-dealer firm naming it Bernard L. Madoff Investment Securities (BLMIS). BLMIS and Gibraltar Securities co-existed as separate businesses for approximately 4 years.

Starting a new securities business took a strong stomach; your firm would be competing with other well established firms on Wall Street. It also took startup money. Bernard committed all $5,000 of his lawn sprinkler profits to the new firm, but much more would be needed. Saul Alpern stepped forward to assist his son-in-law and advanced a $50,000 loan to help capatilize BLMIS.

New broker-dealer businesses are not only difficult to start; they are difficult to grow. BLMIS was competing with large, well known Wall Street firms and needed to be different to survive and innovative to grow.

Bernard Madoff was the right man, at the right time with the right idea. Often described as gregarious (to attract new customers) and an innovator (to create new products), Bernard wanted to be a winner. Victory meant successfully competing with the big firms on Wall Street. To succeed, he needed money and a reputation that would attract customers to his firm.

BLMIS started life trading penny stocks. The firm became a market maker for stocks trading on the Pink Sheets of the National Quotation Bureau. This generated cash, but required significant trading volume in order to generate substantial profits. Trading in the early 1960's was executed by traders working on the exchange floor. Significant trading volume was very labor intensive -meaning it was quite expensive. Madoff conceived an operation that used innovative computer software to advertise bid and ask prices for stocks where his firm was the market maker. Using computer technology to execute trades was revolutionary and allowed BLMIS to successfully compete for large orders with much bigger Wall Street firms. Indeed, the technology that Madoff conceived and BLMIS executed led to the creation of the NASDAQ. This link to being "the father of the NASDAQ" was very important because Madoff used that information to promote his pioneering market skills to attract new clients.

Computer technology allowed Madoff to handle large trading volume efficiently and inexpensively. He now had a technological leg up on the competition.

So how did BLMIS get traders to use his firm to execute their trades? BLMIS was very successful using a process called "payment for order flow." The definition of this strategy is available on SEC.GOV.

> "As a way to attract orders from brokers, some exchanges or market-makers will pay your broker's firm for routing your order to them – perhaps a penny or more per share. This is called "payment for order flow." Payment for order flow is one of the ways your broker's firm can make money from executing your trade. The firm can also make money by internalizing your order."

Traders using BLMIS would not be charged a commission. Instead BLMIS would pay traders to execute their trades with BLMIS rather than using other competing broker-dealer firms. Most Wall Street firms made money by charging traders commissions to execute trades. Now traders were presented with a broker-dealer that would pay them for their orders. How could BLMIS pay traders?

According to a GAO report titled "Decimal Pricing has Contributed to Lower Trading Costs and a More Challenging Trading Environment, GAO-05-535, May 31, 2005"

"In early 2001, U.S. stock and option markets began quoting prices in decimal increments rather than fractions of a dollar. At the same time, the minimum price increment, or tick size, was reduced to a penny on the stock markets and to 10 cents and 5 cents on the option markets. Although many believe that decimal pricing has benefited small individual (retail) investors, concerns have been raised that the smaller tick sizes have made trading more challenging and costly for large institutional investors, including mutual funds and pension plans. In addition, there is concern that the financial livelihood of market intermediaries, such as the broker-dealers that trade on floor-based and electronic markets, has been negatively affected by the lower ticks, potentially altering the roles these firms play in the U.S. capital market. GAO assessed the effect of decimal pricing on retail and institutional investors and on market intermediaries."

For years prices on U.S. stock exchanges were quoted in eighths of a dollar (12.5 cents per share). This 12.5 cents represented the potential profit that a market-maker would receive on each share handled by the firm. The more volume the firm handled the more money it made. Madoff took advantage of this 12.5 cents per share opportunity by sharing part of it with those who executed their order with BLMIS. Traders received a few cents per share while BLMIS retained the largest share of the 12.5 cents as profit to BLMIS.

By paying for the business BLMIS was able to attract very large trading volume and was extremely profitable. At one point BLMIS was the largest market maker on the NASDAQ. At its peak, BLMIS reportedly handled 15% of the total daily trading volume. Processing large trading volume remained a hallmark of BLMIS right up until the end. In 2008 when the end came, BLMIS was still the sixth largest market maker.

Obviously, trading stocks in eighths was enormously profitable for Wall Street. Traders were forced to alter their bid by a minimum of 12.5 cents when adjusting their offering bid price when buying a stock. This leaves a lot of money on the table if a seller were willing to accept a smaller incremental price difference. If traders could change their bid by only a penny their cost for a stock would decline substantially. However, narrowing the spread would reduce broker-dealer profits. Moving to a decimal system was resisted by the brokerage industry because it would narrow the gap from 12.5 cents per share to 1 cent per share. One cent would leave little for profit and nothing for "payment for order flow."

In 1997 stocks began trading in sixteenths (6.2 cents per share). Wall Street profitability suffered to some degree. In 2001 stocks started trading in decimals. This switch to decimals caused a large, almost catastrophic decline in broker dealer profits. NYSE market maker revenues decreased by 50 percent, and NASDAQ market makers reported a 70 percent decrease.

The impact of decimal pricing will be addressed later when discussing reasons why the BLMIS legitimate business developed financial difficulties.

The legitimate part of BLMIS occupied the 19th floor of the Lipstick building in N.Y. According to Bernard Madoff at a roundtable discussion on October 20th, 2007 the firm employed 400 people and handled about $1 trillion dollars of volume each year.

Although Bernard Madoff was the sole stock holder and chief executive of BLMIS, his two sons, Mark and Andrew, actively managed the broker-dealer operation on the 19th floor when they joined the firm in the late 1980s.

BLMIS had an affiliate organization incorporated in the U.K. named Madoff Securities International Ltd (MSIL). Bernard Madoff was the majority shareholder and the Chairman of the Board of Directors for MSIL. His two sons were officers and members of the Board of Directors for MSIL. This U.K. based unit came to play a significant part in the Ponzi scheme which will be described in a later chapter.

The 19th floor operations of BLMIS engaged in two separate types of business operations; market making and proprietary trading. Market making has been described in detail earlier in this chapter and served as the primary money maker for the firm for years – until 2001 when stocks started trading in decimals. Proprietary trading means that the firm, like many of its' Wall Street counterparts, has an internal house account and traded stocks for that account. I have not been able to determine the effectiveness or profitability of the internal proprietary trading operation run by the two sons on the 19th floor.

The lawsuits filed by the SIPC trustee, Irving Picard, provide a wealth of information as to how the legal part of the business functioned and detailed activities of specific employees.

BLMIS was founded by Bernard Madoff in 1960. His two sons did not come on board as employees until the late 1980s. Presumably, Bernard Madoff himself ran both the legal and illegal segments of the business until his sons arrived. Information suggests that Bernard Madoff focused most of his time and attention on the illegal part of the business after his sons largely took responsibility for operations in the broker-dealer business.

Mark and Andrew Madoff were hired by BLMIS to operate the 19th floor where the firm conducted the legal market making and proprietary trading facets of the firm. Their curricula-vitae indicated they were highly educated, well accepted and respected in the Securities industry. Each held significant posts at both BLMIS and MSIL as well as serving on a number of industry boards.

- Mark Madoff (employed by BLMIS in 1986)
  - University of Michigan graduate
  - Co-Director of Trading at BLMIS
  - Controller and Director at MSIL
  - Managed both the Firm's proprietary trading desk and its market-making operations
  - Held at least 3 industry licenses
  - Held many industry positions
    - Chairman of the FINRA Inter-Market Committee
    - Governor of the Securities Traders Association
    - Co-Chair of the STA Trading Committee
    - Member of FINRA Membership Committee and Mutual Fund Task Force
    - President of the STA of New York
    - Chairman of the FINRA Regulation District Ten Business Conduct Committee
    - Chairman of the SIFMA NASDAQ Committee

- Andrew Madoff (employed by BLMIS in 1988)
    - ☐ University of Pennsylvania Wharton Business School graduate
    - ☐ Co-Director of Trading at BLMIS
    - ☐ Controller and Director at MSIL
    - ☐ Managed the trading floor
    - ☐ Directed many audit and compliance projects for BLMIS, including the confirmation and reporting of trades
    - ☐ Held at least 4 industry licenses
    - ☐ Held two industry positions
        - Chairman of the Trading, Trading Issues and Technology, and Decimalization and Market Data Committees and Subcommittees at SIFMA
        - Member of the FINRA District Ten Committee and NASDAQ's Technology Advisory Committee

Bernard Madoff's two sons enjoyed all of the benefits of wealthy parents and took advantage of the opportunities available to those in the upper class. Each attended well respected schools and each was highly trained in the various aspects of finance. These two men could have been successful at any securities firm. They chose to work at BLMIS. And, for some incomprehensible reason, Bernard allowed his sons to work at a firm where he was running a criminal activity.   Some have suggested that keeping the sons isolated on the 19th floor insulated them from the activity on the 17th floor where the father ran his criminal Investment Advisory business. I personally believe that being up two floors in the Lipstick building is simply not enough to distance the sons from what the father was doing. As you read further into this book, you can draw your own conclusions as to the complicity of the sons in the crime of the father.

The illegal Investment Advisory (IA) business

The legitimate part of BLMIS operated on the 19th floor of the Lipstick building in N.Y. Most BLMIS employees worked on this floor. The Investment Advisory (IA) business was located two floors down on the 17th floor. Access to the 17th floor was highly restricted and had some type of key access system.

The legal business is quite easy to understand. Although a pioneer in using computer software to increase trading efficiency and reduce cost; in reality BLMIS was just another quite ordinary broker-dealer.

The IA business was more difficult to understand because Madoff was quite secretive about it. Prior to the collapse I had no reason to question the activities of the IA business nor would I even consider that it might be a total fabrication.

Keep in mind that I did not have any personal relationship with the individual named Bernard Madoff. I had never met the individual nor did I have any knowledge of the inner workings of his IA business. Other than becoming a "customer" in 1992 after the closure of A&B, I had no contact with the firm other than continuing to add funds to my account. My communication "touches" with BLMIS were primarily by mail as a means of adding to the account. In 2006 I originated my one and only withdrawal. A simple phone call to Annette Bongiorno (an employee in the IA department) led to the arrival of a check in just a few days. It was so easy – and the check cleared! Why would it ever enter my mind that the money used to pay the check was nothing more than deposits made by other customers? I thought I made a withdrawal from my account – wouldn't you?

How the IA business worked day-to-day!

From my own statements I know that Madoff traded about six to eight times each year.   My monthly statements looked very much like the sample in Chapter I showing that Madoff followed his stated approach by buying only large cap stocks.   The program never traded in IPOs or other more risky and volatile stocks.   Madoff followed an "all-in" or "all-out" method of investing.   There were about 60 stocks in an account when "all-in", and the account would show only U.S. Treasuries when "all-out."

Madoff had complete discretion over the timing for initiating each round of trading. In keeping with the concept that he was a "brilliant master trader", Madoff, and only Madoff, decided when to buy and when to sell.   Since the composition of the basket of stocks seldom changed you would conclude that Madoff was not a stock picker, he was a market timer. Considering his historical record, he was a very good market timer, the best on Wall Street.

Only Madoff was not a master at market timer – he was a crook!

The entire IA operation was a fraud.   The business ran for decades and produced hundreds of thousands of confirmations and monthly statements showing stock transactions.   None of it was real.   Every single sheet of paper was a ruse to convince investors that their accounts were real and profitable.

In my class I created the power point slide shown below to demonstrate in a simplified form how the IA business worked from day to day. So let's take a journey together into the imaginary world of investing the BLMIS way.

Madoff told most of his IA clients that they could expect a gain of 8% to 12% annually. Since he would execute his all-in/all-out smokescreen about 6-8 times a year Madoff required an average profit of about 1.3% per round trip.

Let's suppose Madoff the master trader miraculously decided "the time to trade is now." He would also decide at the same time on the amount of profit that he wanted to show investors for the "round-trip" in and out of the market. The slide on the next page was taken from my class material and indicates that Madoff decided investors would be granted a 1% profit this time around. Producing a 1% profit is quite easy if you use historical data to look at stock prices over the past few days and compute when the buy should have been placed, and when the sell should occur in order to produce that 1% profit. This process of faking trades would not work if Madoff simply made up the prices – investors might notice something awry if they compared the "fills" on their statement to actual prices reported in the paper. Stock prices could be checked in newspapers and online. Since the reported trades showed prices that were real the process fooled any IA investor who checked the confirmation slips against actual stock prices on the days when Madoff traded. The trick was to use historical data as shown in picture 2 of the slide. Trading activity would now pass the "sniff test."

The third step in the process is to get those thousands of confirmation slips out on a timely basis. Madoff did not provide his customers with online access to their own accounts (this is a red flag for other investors who could fall victim to a similar fraud) so it was necessary to get the confirmations out quickly so as not to raise suspicions. This activity is depicted by picture 3 of the slide.   The fourth picture on the far right shows the satisfied investor who was making a small, but consistent profit on his account. I personally entered each and every Madoff transaction into Quicken and tracked the performance of the account over the years.

This process went on for DECADES.

Lest we forget – the fifth picture on the far left bottom shows "three blind mice" depicting the SEC investigators while all this is going on. The actions, or rather in-actions, of the SEC will be covered in a future chapter.

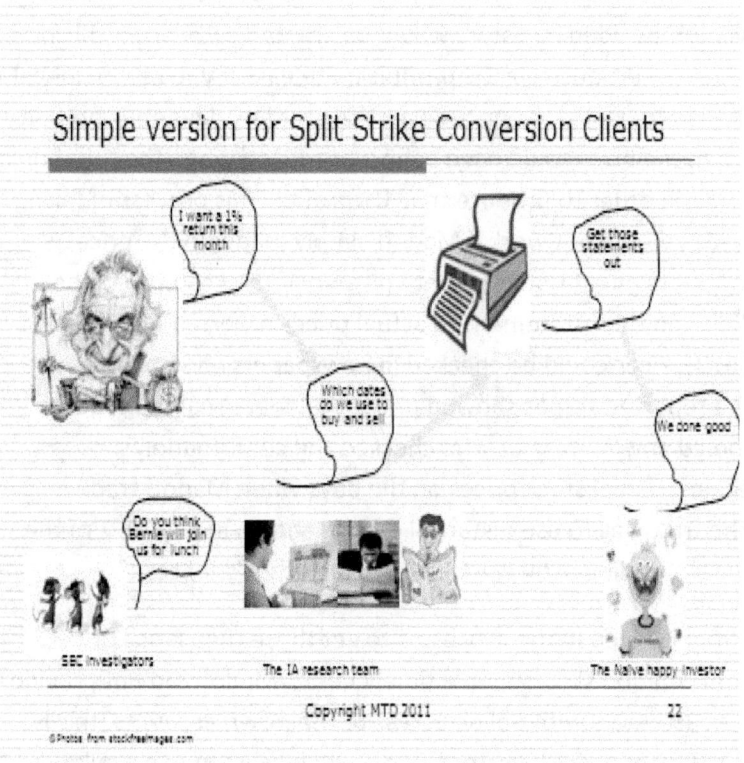

Not all IA clients were created equal

Madoff had a total of about 7,000 IA accounts. The majority of these were split-strike accounts which received annual returns of 8-12%.   Evidence suggests that the great majority of these investors were unaware of any criminal activity.

But Madoff had a second, more nefarious customer type BLMIS called "Non-Split-Strike clients."

There were about 244 of these very special customers. Many were close friends of Madoff and they enjoyed a level of access to Madoff personally as well as communication with his staff that was never available to other customers.

The trustee is suing many of these clients to return some or all of their "gains" suggesting the trustee believes these customers had a level of complicity in the crime warranting "claw back" of funds. Prior to my involvement with litigation involving the dissolution of the Madoff Ponzi scheme I had never heard of "claw back."   This term means that the trustee is attempting to recover funds from those who made withdrawals from their IA account. In the case of those "who knew or should have known" claw back is a means of recovering their "ill-gotten gains."   If you recall the example of Wing-It securities in Chapter III, claw back is also a means of suing innocent investors for withdrawing money they believed was their own. When you read future chapters you will see the impact of claw back litigation against innocents and understand how it impacted their lives, and their health.

Again using a slide from my class, let's take a simplified look at the process for these clients.

As for split-strike clients Madoff would predetermine the return. Only for these clients the numbers far exceeded 8-12% annually. In the Madoff indictment the trustee tells us that these customers were promised returns of at least 45%. These gigantic and totally unbelievable returns have been repeatedly noted by the press. Undoubtedly this reporting led to the stereotype of the greedy investor who must have known. We see this selective behavior by politicians all the time. The political class often take a sound bite or one piece of real information and use it to create a totally distorted and misleading message. Selective reporting by the press, while accurate for some Madoff customers, is not representative of the vast majority of investors.

In the example below, Madoff specified that these preferred investors would receive a 10% return – for one month. Again the staff checked historical records to determine buy and sell dates required to generate this fake return. The time span between buy and sell would likely be much longer to accommodate these larger returns. Of course, these investors would not be spooked by the failure to receive their confirmations in a timely manner. Madoff did not have to fool them – I think they knew exactly what he was doing!

Non-split-strike clients were often handled on an individual basis and amazingly had the option of "requesting" a specific return. Therefore, if a client did not like the return on their statement they simply called the office, told the staff the return they wanted their account to show, and asked for a new statement reporting trades reflecting that return. The REAL stock market does not work that way. It is beyond credulity that these Madoff customers believed the returns were real!

Just how crazy were the returns for these clients? Litigation filed by the trustee against one of these clients provides a vivid example of how high is up when considering returns that Madoff would be willing to provide to his "special friends."

> *"Defendants' accounts regularly earned extraordinary and implausibly high rates of return. ... trading accounts purportedly earned annual rates of return over 100% for four consecutive years, from 1996-1999, inclusive. The*

annual rates of return for these accounts during the period from 1996 to 1999 ranged from a "low" of approximately 120% to a high of over 550%. Nor were these isolated or unusual occurrences; ... for example, purported to earn over 950% in 1999. Indeed, between 1996 and 2007, Defendants' 24 regular trading accounts enjoyed 14 instances of supposed annual returns of more than 100% and 25 in which the annual returns purportedly exceeded 50%. " (SIPA Liquidation No. 08-01789 (BRL))

A careful read of the trustee statement shows that there was no limit to what Madoff would give to one of these preferred clients. Imagine, a 950% return in one year (1999)! Is that a rate of return that any investor would dream about, or is it a nightmare serving only to raise questions about the authenticity of the account?

Although the role of the SEC will be covered in detail in a later chapter, please note the SEC "mice" in the lower left corner of this slide – the agency is totally in the dark and has no clue about what is going on at BLMIS.

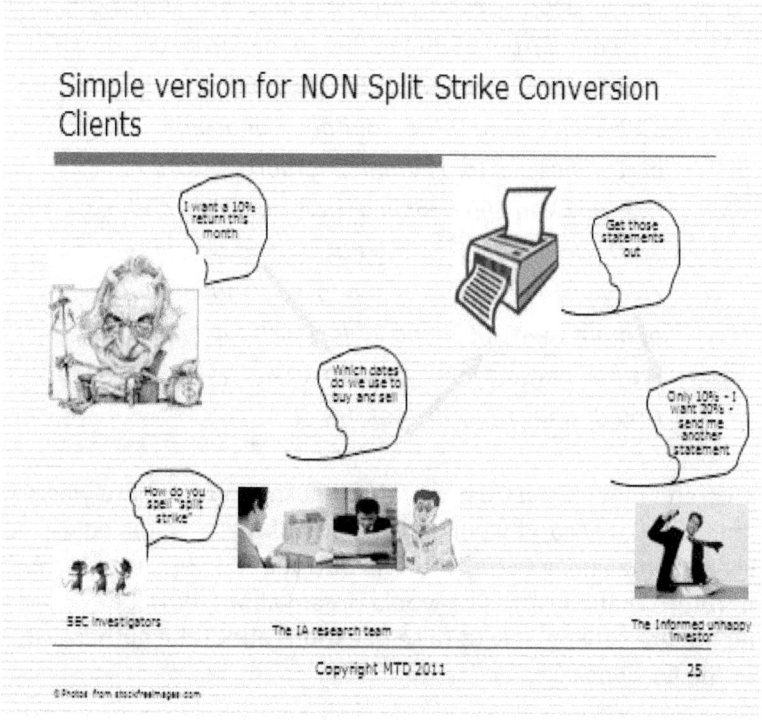

In reality, Madoff did not specify a single rate of return for the non-split strike accounts. Madoff specified different returns for each account or group of accounts. However, the special treatment of these accounts goes beyond the out-of-this-world returns specified by Madoff or requested by his customers. Indeed, clients made profits even before an account was opened. Profits were also reported for accounts that had NEVER been funded with ANY customer money. Madoff was clearly a magician!

The quotes shown below which were taken from the Madoff indictment demonstrates the degree by which customers and Madoff worked in concert to extract money from the Ponzi scheme. Annette Bongiorno was a BLMIS employee who managed the accounts for many non-split-strike clients. She has pleaded not guilty to the charges against her.

MADOFF WAS PERSONALLY INVOLVED IN SETTING THE RETURN FOR SPECIFIC ACCOUNTS

"Madoff communicated the benchmark returns for each account or group of accounts"

TRADING IN THESE ACCOUNTS OCCURRED <u>BEFORE</u> THE ACCOUNTS WERE OPENED

"processed exceptional gains in the IA accounts of the Bongiorno High Net Worth Clients that purportedly occurred months before the IA accounts had been established"

CLIENTS WERE ABLE TO SPEAK WITH IA STAFF AND ACTUALLY RETURN UNWANTED STATEMENTS

"asked Bongiorno High Net Worth Clients to return previously-issued BLMIS account statements so that she could alter them, and often include additional backdated trades"

CLIENTS COULD REQUEST THAT THEIR STATEMENTS REFLECT A SPECIFIC RATE OF RETURN

"received specific instructions from the Bongiorno High Net Worth Clients about the amount of appreciations and gains they wanted to be reflected in their IA accounts"

PROGRAMMERS WROTE SPECIALIZED SOFTWARE TO CREATE ACCOUNTS AND TRADING ACTIVITY MONTHS BEFORE THE ACCOUNTS EXISTED

"used the STMTPRO program, described in paragraph 40 below, to create dozens of IA account statements for the Bongiorno High Net

Worth Clients that contained tens of millions of dollars worth of gains from trades created by BONGIORNO months before the Bongiorno High Net Worth Clients' accounts even had been opened at BLMIS."

ACCOUNTS WERE HANDLED ON AN INDIVIDUAL BASIS

"ANNETTE BONGIORNO, the defendant, asked certain IA Clients to return account statements they previously had received from BLMIS. BONGIORNO, at times, crossed the statements out and wrote new transactions and balances, and other changes, on these statements that were to be included on revised statements."

A careful read of the full 97 page indictment against Madoff reveals multiple comments about the nefarious relationship between Madoff, IA staff and these non-split-strike clients. It is no wonder that the justice system has sued many of the account holders in an attempt to recover assets for Madoff's victims. Many of these "insiders" have pleaded not-guilty and "lawyered-up" to delay any real penalty associated with their activity as a BLMIS IA client.

5 DETAILED INFORMATION ABOUT THE IA BUSINESS

Why start the IA business in the first place!

As I collected data over the past 3 years and came to appreciate the impact of this crime on BLMIS investors (including me) I also pondered Madoff's reasoning for committing such a crime. I had three perplexing questions.

Question 1: The legitimate business for BLMIS was profitable; particularly so when stocks traded in eights. It was a foregone conclusion that this profit opportunity would collapse once stocks traded in decimals. Why not take the big money while spreads were large, then close or sell the firm and retire very wealthy while still a young man? Had Madoff sold the firm in 1995 when the spread was first reduced from eights to sixteenths he would have been only 58 years old. The firm would likely have fetched a very tidy profit for the Madoff family; enough to comfortably last a lifetime for the entire family. It is likely that the value of the firm would continue to decline as the profit opportunities declined when spreads were further reduced to decimals. The thing that made BLMIS special, i.e. paying traders for their business, was going to disappear once the spread disappeared. Madoff must have known this. A smart man would get out before the house burns down and while the business still has sales potential.

The answer to this question is actually self-evident when you realize what Madoff was actually doing on the 19th floor. The fraud started well before margins declined. Madoff could not sell BLMIS because the Ponzi scheme in the IA business had already gotten so large that selling the firm would likely not generate enough money to pay off all the investors and still leave enough for Madoff to exit the business as a wealthy man.

Question 2: This question is something of a subset of question #1. Why start the IA business at all? I can think of only two reasons. The upstart broker-dealer business was not generating enough income to support the aspiring Madoff's lifestyle. Another plausible hypothesis - simply running a broker-dealer business did not adequately feed the inflated ego of the man. Madoff's reputation as one of the best money managers on Wall Street identified him as someone special, a cut above the rest. Had he just run a brokerage, he would have been one among many. Nothing special about that!

Question 3: What would cause a father to put his children at risk? Why would Bernard Madoff let his sons anywhere near his business? By the time Madoff's sons joined BLMIS the illegal part of the business had been in full swing for many years. You have to wonder why Bernard Madoff permitted his only sons to join a business that he knew was a massive criminal enterprise. Ponzi schemes by their very nature eventually become too big and will fail. It is only a matter of time until authorities with handcuffs show up at the door. Why get your family involved in the legal morass that is sure to follow? Madoff tried to protect his sons by having them run the legitimate business on the 19th floor. His sons used this physical separation as a "plausible deniability" crutch telling investigators that they knew nothing of the crime because they had nothing to do with the operation run on a different floor of the building. But the monetary numbers that you will see in later chapters suggest the likelihood of a very different level of awareness and culpability by the family members. My own conclusion is that they clearly knew the essence of what their father was doing – or – they were willfully blind. Either way – the sons made a lot of money off the crimes of the father!

Just how big was the IA business

The size of the investment advisory business was breathtaking. At its peak, the reported value of the statements sent to IA clients was about $64.5 billion. Real investor money deposited into IA accounts was approximately $19 billion. Falsified 1099s reported "gains" account for the difference - about $47.5 billion. Some clients had their money in tax deferred IRA and pension accounts, but the bulk of these gains were taxed as ordinary income by both the Federal IRS and State Departments of Revenue. None of the income reported by BLMIS was classified as long-term capital gains which are taxed at lower preferential rates. Short term capital gains are taxed at the highest rates.

Keep in mind that Madoff clients thought this $47.5 billion in gains was real. Think about it. This was money set aside for homes, education, retirement and estates that would be left to heirs. As in the example of Wing-It Investments, many Madoff investors were already retired and drawing income from their accounts. Consider this scenario - suppose you were retired and living on social security and a pension. Further assume that the pension accounted for 75% of your income. Then one day – the pension stops. What impact would this have on your life? This is analogous to what happened to tens of thousands of Madoff investors whose major source of income consisted of withdrawals from their IA account.

Saul Alpern, Bernard's father-in-law did more than just make a $50,000 loan to jumpstart BLMIS. As a retired CPA, Saul had many business clients which he referred to the firm. These referrals, including Stephen Spielberg, Kevin Bacon and Kyra Sedgewick, were amongst the early clients of BLMIS. These celebrity clients served as a great reference to attract even more wealthy customers to the web being created by Madoff.

The closure of A&B in 1992 returned $450 million to investors. This is likely not the only money that Madoff was managing, but for purposes of discussing the growth of funds that Madoff handled let's assume this represented the total under management in 1992. The trustee reported the value of all statements produced by Madoff as of 11/30/2008 was $64.5 billion.

A Ponzi scheme requires a steady flow of new money to remain viable. From 1992 to 2008 the amount of money involved in the scheme (including falsified profits) increased from $450 million to $64.5 billion, more than 140 times larger over a period of 16 years. An alternative approach that includes counting only "real" money and removing the false gains from the computation still yields an incredible increase in deposits which increased from $450 million to $19 billion; the fund grew 38 times larger over 16 years.

Sixty-five BILLION ($65,000,000,000); you can count the zeroes but it is almost impossible to grasp the scope of such a large number. When you compare Madoff to other recent financial crimes the sheer size of Madoff's crime is breathtaking. Madoff stole an order of magnitude more from his investors than perpetrators of other recent crimes against innocent investors that will be discussed in later chapters.

Bernard Madoff - $65 billion (2008)

Allen Stanford - $7 billion. (2008)

MF Global – $1.7 billion. (2011-2012)

PFGBest - $230 million (2012)

Joseph Forte - $75 million (2009)

Every one of these schemes causes immense damage not only to investor assets but also wreaks havoc on confidence in the system. Every investor thought the only risk they accepted was market losses – fraud, theft, deception – I am certain these issues never entered their mind. Confidence in the system will continue to erode as more American investors find out what happened (as you are by reading this book). Market participation is already on the decline as investors find the system stilted in favor of insiders. With fraud becoming more of an issue, investors will be even less willing to participate in the U.S. securities market. It is troubling enough to risk investing in a system which is biased against you; it is quite another to accept that major players are willing to commit wholesale fraud against their own customers. It appears that many on Wall Street may have skipped the course on "business ethics" when attending school and failed to learn the meaning of "fiduciary responsibility" and putting their client first.

John Nyaradi wrote an article on July 18, 2012, (marketwatch.com) titled "Swimming with sharks as scandals mount"

> *"Investors are now swimming with sharks as scandal after scandal rocks the financial sector.*
>
> *Many investors have lost confidence in the system and are hiding under their beds, while those still playing wonder if there is any chance of winning what many perceive to be a manipulated game. "*

The more investors feel they are playing in a gamed system; the less likely they will be to participate. One time tested approach to cheating investors employed by many in the piranha-infested world of penny stock boiler rooms is to manipulate price using "pump and dump" transactions of worthless stocks. Madoff chose not to participate in such a nefarious act as price manipulation. He carried his crime out using a more creative approach - by simply producing fake reports with real prices for otherwise valuable stocks.

Timeline for the Ponzi scheme

BLMIS began business as a broker-dealer in 1959. Apparently, the legitimate broker dealer business did not provide sufficient income to meet the lofty expectations of the owner. It is not precisely clear when Madoff started to accept money from clients offering to serve as their Investment Advisor. Madoff himself stated that it began in the 1990s. As has been proven by his guilty plea, there is almost NO connection between Madoff and truth. Therefore, we have to look to other sources to discern when the scheme started.

Information reported on en.wikipedia.org/wiki/Bernard_Madoff provides direction for estimates for when Madoff started accepting money from investors.

> *"Madoff said he began the Ponzi scheme in the early 1990s. However, federal investigators believe the fraud began as early as the 1970s, and those charged with recovering the missing money believe the investment operation may never have been legitimate"*

David Kugel, a trader who worked at BLMIS for almost four decades, was sued by SIPC under case # 08-01789 (BRL). Two paragraphs under the "Nature of Proceeding" in this lawsuit indicate the role played by Mr. Kugel in the early life of the BLMIS Investment Advisory business.

> *"Kugel worked for BLMIS for nearly 40 years. He started at BLMIS in 1970 after spending approximately a year as an assistant trader with another Wall Street firm where he was involved primarily in trading convertible securities. When he joined BLMIS, Kugel continued to trade in convertible securities, which included making a market in such securities and engaging in an arbitrage trading strategy involving the purchase of convertible securities and the short sale of the related common stock. BLMIS employees referred to this strategy generally as the "arbitrage" strategy.*
>
> *BLMIS purportedly employed a very similar convertible arbitrage strategy <u>in the investment advisory side of its business, and Kugel played a critical role here as well</u>. From as early as the*

*mid-1970s to as late as 1998, BLMIS fraudulently
misrepresented to at least 1,300 of its
investment advisory customers that their BLMIS
accounts were invested in a convertible
arbitrage strategy when in reality their money
was never invested by BLMIS. <u>Kugel very likely
was the architect of this fraudulent strategy</u>.
Over the years, Kugel structured the fraudulent
trades which were allocated between the
accounts held by BLMIS investors. The pricing
that Kugel used in the purported trades often
was based on pure hindsight; in other instances,
his pricing was fabricated to generate
predetermined returns for BLMIS investors."*

Many of these allegations became factual when on November
16, 2011 David Kugel pleaded guilty to the following charges in
the US District Court of Southern NY (case # 54 10 Cr. 228 (LTS)).

1. A conspiracy beginning in the early 1970s through
    December 2008 to commit securities fraud, falsify records of a
    broker-dealer, and falsify records of an investment adviser
    at BLMIS by participating with other co-conspirators in
    the creation of fake trades used to deceive the clients of
    BLMIS's Investment Advisory business
2. A conspiracy to commit bank fraud
3. Securities fraud
4. Falsifying records of a broker-dealer
5. Falsifying records of an investment adviser
6. Bank fraud

An Associated Press article on November 21, 2011 provides
additional insight into the role of David Kugel in the Madoff
fraud. In spite of his direct involvement in the crime, Kugel was
able to negotiate a plea bargain with authorities to lessen the
impact of penalties against him. Sometimes it is easier for

authorities to accept a plea to lesser charges in order to gain cooperation in getting "the bigger fish." Sometimes it is easier to accept the plea than try to prove the charges in a court of law. David Kugel accomplished both objectives with his plea arrangement.

"David Kugel pleaded guilty in US District Court in Manhattan to conspiracy, securities fraud, bank fraud, falsifying business records and falsifying the books of an investment adviser, charges that carry a potential penalty of up to 85 years in prison. A cooperation deal with prosecutors that leaves Kugel free on $3 million bail would earn him leniency at a sentencing tentatively scheduled for May 4. As part of the plea, he agreed to forfeit $3.5 million to the government.

The 66-year-old Kugel told Judge Laura Taylor Swain that he was engaging in fraud in the private investment wing of Madoff's Manhattan-based business in the early 1970s.

He said he was "deeply sorry."

"I want the court to know I will do all I can to cooperate with the government," Kugel, of Manhasset, said at the outset of a statement he gave describing his fraud.

He said it stretched from the early 1970s to Dec. 11, 2008, when Madoff revealed that a business he started in the 1960s had turned into a giant Ponzi scheme, causing the loss of $19.5 billion invested by thousands of people and institutions, including charities.

> *But Kugel said he and other Madoff employees*
> *were faking trades in the 1970s to give "the*
> *appearance of profitable trades when, in fact, no*
> *trading had occurred."*

Now we have quite a bit of new information about when the fraud started with the information provided by an early trader who falsified trading tickets for the fraudulent IA business. Let's try to understand David Kugel's role in the Madoff scandal.

1. Kugel served as a supervisory trader in the proprietary trading business of BLMIS. He worked on the 19th floor thereby breaking the firewall between the legitimate and illegal businesses.
2. Kugel was engaged in the deception beginning in the early 1970s; right after he began working for the firm. This was nearly 15 years before Madoff tells us the fraud started.
3. By the early 1990s the 17th floor was fully functioning and processing "trades" for IA accounts. Yet, for some unexplained reason, Kugel continued to falsify trades on the 19th floor until 2008.
4. The allegations suggest that Kugel may have been the designer of the entire fraudulent process. Madoff simply perfected and automated the process on the 17th floor.
5. Kugel confirms the process of using historical data to report trades to customers was used from the very beginning.
6. Kugel confirms that "others" were involved in perpetrating the fraud; again in direct contrast with Madoff's statement that he alone conceived, designed and operated the entire operation.

With what we know so far we can begin building a timeline for the Madoff fraud. The firm was founded in 1959. From David Kugel we can date his participation in the fraud to 1970. Federal investigators also indicate Madoff likely started in the

1970s, just a few years after the firm was founded. Since the firm started as a penny stock broker dealer and there is no reliable information as to when Madoff started to manage money – one could easily conclude that the IA business was NEVER legitimate.

Ponzi schemes need a steady supply of new money to survive. The SEC investigation of Avellino and Bienes in 1992 indicates that this Ponzi scheme was worth about $450m – all of which was returned to investors. Much of this money went back to Madoff as he solicited those investors for inclusion in the IA program at BLMIS. I have not uncovered information that there were significant other "feeder funds" other than A&B before 1992. We do know that the value of IA "investments" grew from $450 million in 1992 to $65 billion in 2008. Throughout this book we will now begin to fill in the blanks for other significant events occurring between 1992 and 2008.

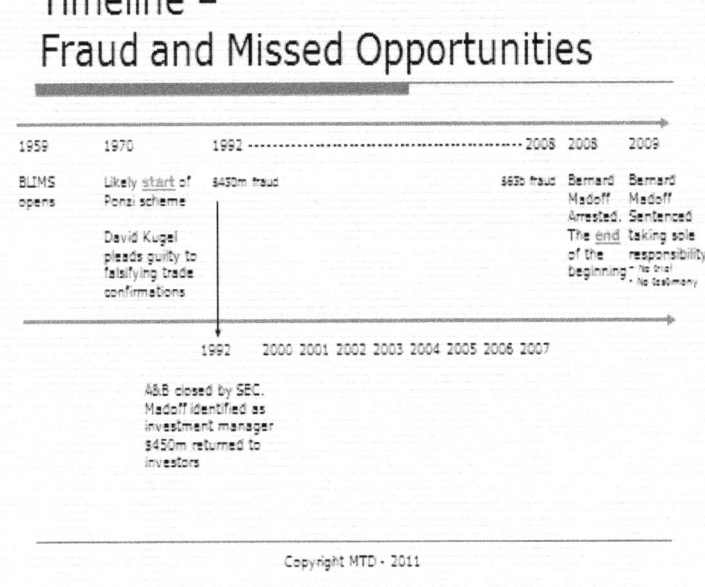

Timeline –
Fraud and Missed Opportunities

1959	1970	1992 2008	2008	2009
BLMS opens	Likely start of Ponzi scheme	$450m fraud	$65b fraud	Bernard Madoff Arrested. The end of the beginning	Bernard Madoff Sentenced taking sole responsibility - No trial - No testimony
	David Kugel pleads guilty to falsifying trade confirmations				

1992   2000 2001 2002 2003 2004 2005 2006 2007

A&B closed by SEC.
Madoff identified as
investment manager
$450m returned to
investors

Copyright MTD · 2011

"Oh what a tangled web we weave" - How did Madoff attract so many to the IA business

When Bernard Madoff said he "made a lot of money for a lot of people" he was not kidding. He should have added that "the people" he was talking about were not the majority of his investors, it was his sales force and preferred investors.

Let's take a look at the credentials of Bernard Madoff. They are impressive and play a significant role in attracting customers to his Investment Advisory business.

- ☐ Bernard Madoff's credentials
    - ■ Planned and developed the innovative computer technology that led to the creation of the NASDAQ
    - ■ Two-time Chairman of the Board of Directors of the NASDAQ
    - ■ On the Board of Governors of the NASD (National Association of Securities Dealers)
    - ■ On the Board of Directors of the Securities Industry Association, which merged with the Bond Market Association in 2006 to form SIFMA (Securities Industry and Financial Markets Association)
    - ■ Frequent consultant to the SEC
    - ■ Considered for the post of Treasury Secretary in the 1990s (according to Madoff)
    - ■ Involved in politics: Since 1991, Madoff contributed about $240,000 to federal candidates, parties and committees including $25,000 a year to the Democratic Senatorial Committee. He also contributed to BOTH the Democratic and Republican Conventions. Contributions to individuals was 88% Democratic; 12% Republican
    - ■ Major philanthropist – sat on the boards of many non-profit institutions, many of which trusted

their endowments to BLMIS (most of that money
is gone and many charities have closed); donated
$6m to lymphoma research (of course, Madoff
was donating money that he stole from others)

Madoff's role and reputation in the securities industry
progressed over a period of years.   The crime started long
before many of Madoff's industry positions and honorable
mentions occurred.   How did he attract those initial clients and
how did he put the pieces together to grow into the largest
financial crime in history?

Saul Alpern, Bernard's father-in-law, provided two indispensable
assets for Bernard Madoff.   He assured the startup had capital
by loaning the firm $50,000.   And, as a retired CPA, he opened
the door to a wealthy client base by vouching for his son-in-law.
These early referrals included many of the Hollywood rich and
famous.   Later notable investors include U.S. Senator Frank
Lautenberg.   Success recruiting well known customers breeds
more success attracting others to invest.   Networking in any
business is an integral part of growth and these clients
undoubtedly served as a reference item to solicit additional
business.   If Madoff was to grow - he had to deliver!   Madoff
had to show consistency and a rate of return consistent with the
definition of a "great money manager."   Well, if the whole IA
business is a fake - those two objectives were easy to reach – all
he had to do was make the numbers up!

Madoff's claim that he ran the entire operation himself is even
more laughable when considering the sheer scope of the
business. The total number of clients in the IA business is
measured in the tens, perhaps even hundreds, of thousands.
The octopus of Madoff's IA business extended its tentacles well
beyond the shores of the U.S. Madoff's business circumvented
the globe into Europe and Asia.   Clearly a global business needs
a global network to attract and service clients.

David Kugel provided the fake paperwork for early clients; and
the trade tickets were done by hand.   The volume that could be

manually handled by one person would limit any significant growth potential for the business. The theft process just had to be automated.

Once the computerized system was in place the IA business was free to grow by an order of magnitude; after all, computers are really good at churning out a lot of paper.

It has been reported that Madoff required a minimum investment in order to open an individual account. But there are only so many individuals that could meet those minimums. To further expand the pool of available investors Madoff developed a strategy allowing individuals to group together and invest as a single entity through a so-called "feeder fund." A feeder fund is similar to a mutual fund in that it takes money from a large number of investors, uses that money to buy shares in a fund, and that fund uses the money to buy individual stocks. The statement provided to investors shows shares of the fund rather than naming the actual securities that were purchased.

The "feeder sales force" allowed Madoff to significantly increase the number of investors snared by his web. To encourage effort to attract new customers and silence to maintain concealment of the scam, Madoff needed a sales force he could trust. Money can buy trust. Pay them enough to maintain their loyalty and preserve the secrecy of the firm's activities. Of course, by knowing participating in a fraud, these feeder fund employees open themselves to criminal prosecution. After Madoff was arrested, these employees, like everyone else involved, claimed they knew nothing and were duped by Madoff.

A chart from the course shows the many branches from the large tree that fed money to Madoff's IA business. The diagram which is admittedly difficult to read, was produced by conciselearning.com and shows the complexity and reach of the World-Wide-Web (a completely new meaning for the letters WWW) created by Madoff to gather $19 billion of investor money.

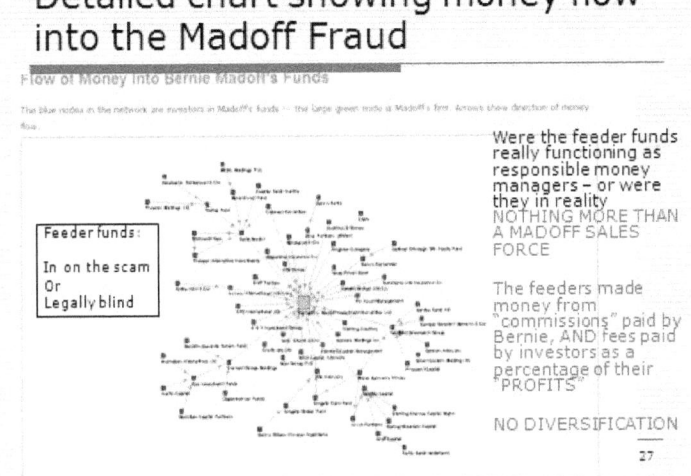

Detailed chart showing money flow into the Madoff Fraud

Remember that a Ponzi scheme is doomed to eventual failure. The moment that redemption requests exceed new investor deposits the scheme goes onto life support. Madoff needed a steady and growing supply of new investors. And he needed a seemingly independent sales force to approach new clients.

To generate those new funds Madoff created many feeder funds that were scattered throughout the U.S., Europe and Asia. As you can see in the chart above, Madoff's network was vast.

A sampling of some of the larger cash generators for Madoff provides an insight into how Madoff and his cohorts were able to find investors to support the Ponzi scheme. Below is a list of just a few of them along with some detail about their role in feeding the Madoff beast. The various complaints filed by the trustee provide a rich source of information about how Madoff worked with these individuals to continue to provide the life blood of a Ponzi scheme – new investor money.

~1988: Fairfield Greenwich Group – Raised approximately $4.5 billion (about 24% of all IA investments)

According to the complaint filed by the trustee, this firm served a significant role in supporting the scheme including coordinating communication with the SEC while soliciting new clients to the firm.

> *"worked closely with Madoff and/or BLMIS throughout a nearly twenty year relationship, including, but not limited to: (1) coordinating responses to United States Securities Exchange Commission investigations of BLMIS, (2) collaborating in SEC filings, and (3) obtaining new money used by BLMIS to perpetuate his Ponzi scheme"*

Fairfield employees were well compensated for their efforts.

> *"the investment manager of the Defendant funds reaped massive fees, in excess of hundreds of millions of dollars, purportedly for investment performance which has proven to be nothing but fiction."*

Fairfield was a professional money management firm.   As with any firm with a fiduciary responsibility to customers, an investor would expect that Fairfield would not only vet investment vehicles, but would also continually monitor trading activity and performance.   Madoff must have been very convincing if we are to believe that Fairfield executives did any due diligence verification of BLMIS and yet discovered nothing of the fraud. The trustee clearly has drawn a different conclusion accusing Fairfield of failure to investigate investments with Madoff in each of these five areas.

1. "HIGH AND UNUSUALLY CONSISTENT RETURNS"
   a. Investment professionals should have considered the consistency of the returns as a red flag
2. "PRICES OUTSIDE DAILY RANGE"
   a. There were a number of trades reported to Fairfield where the price reported was outside the range for that stock on that day
3. "PURPORTED TRADES SETTLED ON WEEKENDS/HOLIDAYS"
   a. Trades were reported to have occurred on days when the market was not open
4. "UNREALISTICALLY HIGH VOLUMES OF EQUITIES TRADING"
   a. Trading volume for a particular stock reported to Fairfield was higher than the daily trading volume for that security
5. "OPTIONS IN EXCESS OF THE CBOE MARKET"
   a. Madoff hedged his reported stock trades with options. Fairfield received reports of a higher level of option trading than existed on the total exchange

If the trustee claims are accurate, the only conclusion one could draw is that Fairfield was either negligent or complicit. Fairfield was not exposed to a single smoking gun, it was exposed to many. Imagine, prices reported that were outside the daily trading range, more trading activity than existed on a given day, trades settling on days when the market was not open – all available to Fairfield, all apparently ignored. It is clear that Madoff was not nearly as careful with the paperwork sent to this feeder fund as he was with individual account holders.

Fairfield did very little to ensure the safety of their customers money. The firm simply took client money, gave it to Madoff, and received hundreds of millions in payments from Madoff in compensation for their efforts not to manage money, but to raise it for BLMIS to manage.

Do you wonder if your investment advisor might be doing the same?

Fairfield managers and employees claim they knew nothing of the scam!

1985: Cohmad – Raised $1.1 billion (about 6% of all IA investments)

Cohmad was formed by Madoff and Sonny Cohn (a friend and former neighbor). The name Cohmad was derived by combining the first three letters of the surnames of the founders – COH for Cohn, and MAD for Madoff - thus yielding the word "Cohmad." The relationship between Cohmad and BLMIS is incestuous at best. What kind of objectivity would a fund management firm have when the firm directs ALL of their client's money to one of the founders?

Not only did the mouse (Cohmad) and the cat (BLMIS) co-exist in name, but the two firms also occupied the same physical space and employees. Cohmad did not have its own office space, computer systems or operational employees. Conveniently, Cohmad was located on the 18th floor of the Lipstick building in N.Y.; sandwiched in-between the 19th floor where the market-making business was located and the 17th floor where the IA business conducted operations. Although Cohmad ostensibly leased this space from BLMIS, there is no evidence that Cohmad ever paid any rent to the firm.

Suspiciously for a firm that SHOULD have been independent, the Cohn's had key access to the 17th floor; a benefit that was not offered to regular employees of BLMIS nor to other feeder fund managers.

"Despite the fact that they were ostensibly separate companies, the connections between Cohmad and BLMIS were so pervasive that they acted in many respects as interconnected arms of the same enterprise. Cohmad, whose employees both functioned and were compensated as though they were BLMIS representatives, was founded by Madoff and his friend and former neighbor, Maurice "Sonny" Cohn. Cohmad - a name fashioned out of the first three letters of the names "Cohn" and "Madoff" - had its New York offices entirely within BLMIS' premises and even utilized BLMIS' employees and computer network. Cohmad's primary business was directed towards helping BLMIS recruit an ever-expanding list of high-net-worth clients into the Ponzi scheme, and ultimately Cohmad and its registered representatives diverted several billion dollars to Madoff."

While it may have appeared to be an independent business; in reality Cohmad served only ONE purpose – to funnel client money to the Madoff IA business. Over 90% of Cohmad's income came in the form of compensation and payments from BLMIS.

"90% of Cohmad's reported income resulted from the continual referral of victims to BLMIS"

Not only did Cohmad receive virtually ALL of its income from BLMIS, it received a LOT of money.

> *"Defendants collectively profited from the Madoff Ponzi scheme to the tune of several hundred million dollars, through conduct that they knew or should have known was inconsistent with legitimate or credible securities or broker-dealer business activities."*

BLMIS made payments to Cohmad every month. The table below shows just how much money Cohmad received for providing the single service of funneling client money to Madoff. In 12 years (1996 to 2008), the payments totaled **$98,448,678.84**.

Year	Amount
1996	$4,789,019.62
1997	$7,378,789.26
1998	$8,098,228.23
1999	$9,874,438.90
2000	$10,415,793.21
2001	$9,892,273.82
2002	$10,905,265.27
2003	$9,462,247.47
2004	$6,745,439.44
2005	$7,239,978.09
2006	$6,449,342.84
2007	$4,583,267.63
2008	$2,614,595.06
TOTAL:	**$98,448,678.84**

These payments to Cohmad were in the form of "commissions." Cohmad had a sales force that actually did the work of soliciting clients. This commission would be split between Cohmad and the sales force.

Many real investment advisors are compensated based on a percentage of the money under management; often in the range of .5% to 1.5%. If the manger fee is based on a percentage of the total under management, then accounts that make money generate larger payments. The manager benefits by making money for a client since the base for the commission or management fee grows over time.

Conversely, the commission to the Cohmad sales force was based only on the CASH value of customer accounts. Cohmad paid NO additional commissions based on the reported value of the accounts which included investment gains.

There is a reason Cohmad did not pay the sales force using account values including investment profits. The gains were all faked, Cohmad knew it and the sales force knew it too! Cohmad maintained records which showed the net value of each account – completely discounting any gains reported to investors. Other than awareness that the whole thing was a fraud – why would Cohmad maintain records ignoring account gains?

Commission payments to Cohmad were not the only raid on the piggy bank holding BLMIS IA investor funds. BLMIS also made additional payments to one of the founders, Sonny Cohn who received an additional **$14,601,213.15** during the seven years from 2002 through 2008.

Year	Amount
2002	$2,437,165.00
2003	$2,350,600.00
2004	$1,882,831.05
2005	$1,930,617.10
2006	$2,000,000.00
2007	$2,000,000.00
2008	$2,000,000.00
Total	**$14,601,213.15**

Like other corporations, Cohmad had a board of directors. The directors and officers of Cohmad included many family members of both Bernard Madoff and Sonny Cohn. Considering the business activities of Cohmad, it is not surprising that this was not an independent board but one closely held and controlled likely to ensure a level of secrecy from the outside world. In addition to the two founders, directors and officers include:

Peter Madoff (Madoff's brother)

Milton Cohn (Sonny's brother)

Marcia Cohn (Sonny's daughter)

Shana Madoff (Peter Madoff's daughter) was named as compliance counsel

My conclusion is that Cohmad was nothing more than a front to accumulate additional investor money for the Ponzi scheme.

The Cohn's claim they knew nothing of the scam! Board members Peter and Shana Madoff claim they knew nothing of the scam!

1990: Avellino & Bienes Raised $450m (about 2% of all IA investments)

This was one of the early recruiters of customers to Madoff. As a result of the SEC investigation, A&B was closed and all money, including gains, was returned to investors. Madoff contacted many of these investors offering them the opportunity to open an individual account with his IA business.

The owners of A&B were compensated in the form of a commission that was based on the amount of money the firm raised for Madoff.

Avellino and Bienes claim they knew nothing of the scam!

1994: Bank Medici – Raised $9.1 billion (about 46% of all IA investments)

Bernard Madoff met Sonja Kohn in 1985. Two years later Kohn formed "Medici Enterprise" and began soliciting customers for the Madoff Ponzi scheme. In 1994, Sonja Kohn formed Bank Medici, an Austrian bank which the trustee contends was nothing more than a conduit setup for the sole purpose of funneling money to Mr. Madoff through several feeder funds. Kohn and Madoff shared a common goal – separating individuals from their money!

> *"In Sonja Kohn, Madoff found a criminal soul mate, whose greed and dishonest inventiveness equaled his own.* Sonja Kohn went by many names and operated under many guises, creating an international network of spurious investment entities and masterminding an illegal scheme not only to support the Madoff fraud, but also to enrich herself, her family, and the largest banks in Austria and Italy"

Sonja Kohn expanded the reach of Madoff beyond the shores of the U.S. into Europe and beyond. Customers, whom I prefer to call victims, were found in the U.K., Russia, France, Germany, Austria, Italy, Gibraltar and many, many other countries.

Although the Medici Enterprise had many different funds ostensibly with different investment objectives and holding, it is abundantly clear that all served only one purpose – to grow Madoff's IA business. Funds created by Sonja include the following: Primeo Fund, Ltd., Thema International Fund plc, Herald Fund SPC, Alpha Prime Fund Ltd., and Senator Fund Ltd. In practice, all investor funds, regardless of the Medici Fund name, were 100% invested with BLMIS.

Sonja Kohn and Bank Medici were major players in raising money for Madoff. In the 199 page complaint the trustee claimed that about half the fraud's stolen funds — $9.1 billion out of an estimated $19.6 billion — was directly attributable to Ms. Kohn, her family members and their elaborate portfolio of feeder funds.

Unlike many of the non-split-strike investors who had their own personal accounts with the IA business (remember that these investors were able to specify the returns they desired for their accounts), Kohn did not have a personal BLMIS account. That does not mean that Kohn did not make millions. Like so many others who worked to feed the appetite of the growing beast, Sonja Kohn and her associates were extremely well compensated. I have not been able to determine exactly how much Kohn received by fronting for Madoff, but the trustee reports Kohn received at least $62 million in payments from BLMIS in 2007 and 2008 alone. These payments were disguised as something other than commission for funneling money to Madoff. Many of the invoices listed fictional services such as "market research." In reality the two year payment of $62 million represented kickbacks for finding investors for the IA business.

The trustee complaint tells us quite a bit about the incestuous relationship between Madoff and Kohn.

> *"For more than twenty years, Kohn masterminded a vast illegal scheme (the "Illegal Scheme") to exploit her privileged relationship with Madoff to feed over $9.1 billion of other people's money into his Ponzi scheme. The Illegal Scheme enriched Kohn, her family, and scores of other individuals and entities, including the largest banks in Austria and Italy, at the expense of the BLMIS estate and on the backs of Madoff's victims.*
>
> *To potential BLMIS investors, Kohn held herself out as extremely close to Madoff and suggested*

that their special relationship yielded special returns on investments through BLMIS. In fact, Madoff secretly paid Kohn in exchange for feeding money into the Ponzi scheme. This agreement between Kohn and Madoff was kept secret, and was unknown even to many within BLMIS. All the while, Kohn operated as a BLMIS insider and knew that Madoff was a fraud.

As Kohn built the Medici Enterprise into a wholesale operation, Madoff secretly paid Kohn at least $62 million in secret kickbacks for bringing investors into BLMIS. On information and belief, Madoff paid Kohn far more. Madoff kept internal records that noted which accounts were attributable to Kohn. Madoff appears to have destroyed these records of his agreement with Kohn before he confessed on December 11, 2008. Certain former employees, however, kept copies of such records."

Kohn was an insider and was undoubtedly aware of the liquidity crisis of 2008 and the associated financial difficulties Madoff experienced meeting customer redemptions requests. Evidence that she knew the scheme was collapsing manifests itself in her actions in November of 2008, just weeks before Madoff's arrest. Kohn withdrew $536 million from BLMIS accounts and moved it to Bank Medici. This was followed in early December by Kohn withdrawing ALL of her family's personal assets from the bank thus limiting law enforcements ability to recover assets for victims of the illegal scheme. The money that Kohn withdrew represented much of what was left in Madoff's JP Morgan Chase account. It seems likely that Kohn decided to grab what was left before the scheme totally unraveled leaving almost nothing in the piggy bank for innocent investors. Madoff had almost $500 million remaining – Kohn took $423 million for herself and her family.

"As the Ponzi scheme approached its inevitable collapse on December 11, 2008, Kohn conspired to protect herself, her family, and key members of the Medici Enterprise. In the months leading up to and after Madoff's confession, Kohn directed certain members of the Medici Enterprise to conceal the proceeds of the Illegal Scheme, including stolen Customer Property.

Just before Madoff confessed, Kohn directed Herald Fund to withdraw $536 million from BLMIS, including $423 million in one transfer on November 4, 2008. Kohn's associate, Giefing, executed Herald Fund's withdrawal on behalf of Kohn. BLMIS's bank account at J.P. Morgan Chase held approximately $500 million the day before Herald Fund's $423 million withdrawal. Herald Fund withdrew the other $113 million just a month before. This $536 million is almost sixteen times the total that Herald Fund had ever withdrawn before.

On information and belief, Kohn and her husband maintained personal bank accounts at Bank Medici. Just days before Madoff confessed, Kohn directed her husband to withdraw all of their personal assets from any member of the Medici Enterprise, including Bank Austria, that had the potential to be exposed to liability for its participation in the Illegal Scheme."

So where is Kohn today?   Not in the US where she would be within reach of the Justice system.   But also not out of business as she continues to run Medici Enterprise from Europe.   One also has to question why the European authorities have not closed Medici. I also question why she is not in jail, serving time, just like Madoff. Will you be her next victim?

> *"On information and belief, Kohn has not returned to New York (or the United States) since Madoff confessed. Rather, she has conducted and continues to conduct the affairs of the Medici Enterprise from Europe and elsewhere through her family and her New York instrumentalities Eurovaleur and Infovaleur."*

Sonja Kohn and others employed at Medici Enterprises claim they knew nothing of the scam!

1994: Chaise Funds

Stanley Chais was a personal friend of Bernard Madoff for at least 30 years. Like other insiders he had special access to Madoff and his phone number was on Madoff's speed dial.

According to the complaint filed by the trustee, Stanley Chais was an unregistered investment advisor who had both a business and social relationship with Bernard Madoff since at least the early 1970s. He has been called "the Beverly Hills Money Manager" for his role in feeding Madoff's scheme.

Chais made money from the Madoff scheme in two ways; he had his own personal accounts with Madoff, and he earned a commission on those he brought into the Madoff fold by investing in the Chais Funds.

Do you see a pattern here? Kohn had many funds all invested with Madoff; and so did Chais. Apparently Madoff and his cohorts found something that worked – so he replicated the process over and over again. I believe the ruse was meant to dupe investors into thinking there were many funds with different managers and investment options – but in reality, it was ALL Bernie!

In addition to the funds where Chais took other investors money, he also drank from the same cup as the other 244 "special investors." Chais opened more than 60 personal and family accounts with Madoff.   These were of the non-split-strike variety which incorporate very special benefits not available to most investors. In keeping with the performance of other accounts of this type, the returns for the personal Chais accounts were unrealistically high. While the trustee reports an average annual return of 20% to 24% for those invested in the regular Chais Funds he tells us that Stanley Chais did even better in his personal accounts. Personal Chais IA accounts earned approximately 40% annually. Madoff reported to Chais that one year his personal accounts returned 300%.

Of course, these "gains" were false since there was no real trading for any IA account. These fantastic returns were simply a means of transferring deposits from other investors to accounts setup for the personal benefit of Stanley Chais and friends.

From 1995 until the Ponzi scheme collapse in 2008 Chais removed at least $1 billion from his personal accounts.   For an investment advisor with real trading experience Chais must have been amazed at the returns his accounts "earned" with Madoff. I chose to believe that he knew the whole operation was a scam!

> *"Chais has been closely associated with Madoff on both a business and social level since at least the 1970s. Stanley Chais ("Chais") was a beneficiary of this Ponzi scheme for at least thirty years.*

Defendant Chais is an unregistered investment advisor formerly based in Beverly Hills who invested in BLMIS over many decades through more than 60 entity and/or personal accounts.

Regular trading accounts for investment funds managed by Chais received unrealistically high and consistent annual returns of between 20% and 24%, with only three months of purported negative returns over 144 months of purported trading. At the same time, Chais' own family and corporate accounts reported even higher returns, sometimes in excess of 100%—and even 300%— per year, with a combined average annual return approaching 40%."

Revenue to Chais went beyond simply getting these unrealistic returns for his own personal accounts.   Chais also managed the "Chais Funds" for other investors.   Portraying himself as a professional investment advisor Chais commanded a significant portion of the "returns" as a management fee from his investors. The arrangement called for Chais to receive a fee of 25% of all earnings which exceed 10% annually.   Since Madoff told investors they were getting 20-24%, this "management fee" generated significant income for Chais – he was getting 3% of all reported income (25% of everything over 10% or about 25% of 12%).   This is WAY outside the range of what most investment advisors charge customers.   And for this – Chais did NOTHING but give the money to Madoff. As with Fairfield, there was no attempt to verify anything that Madoff was doing. For a "sophisticated investor", Chais either knew it was a fake or he deliberately chose to ignore the obvious fact that his personal accounts were doing twice as well as the money under management by Bernie for his investors.

"Defendant Chais managed the assets of the Chais Funds, which management included directing where those assets were to be invested, and Chais was paid or received substantial fees in connection with his management duties.

Defendant Chais is a sophisticated investor who acts as a professional investment advisor in his capacity as general partner of the Chais Funds. According to complaints filed by Chais Fund investors and Chais Fund records held or obtained by BLMIS, Chais collected fees equal to 25% of each Chais Fund's entire net profit for every calendar year in which profits exceeded 10% -- which has occurred every calendar year since at least 1996. Chais received these fees in consideration for exercising his purported skill and judgment in managing investments. Chais has reportedly known Madoff for decades and has been invested in BLMIS since at least the 1970s. Chais' telephone number appears as the first speed dial entry on a telephone list at BLMIS. He therefore enjoyed unusually intimate access to Madoff, allowing him an opportunity to gain special access to extensive information about the operations of BLMIS."

So how did Chais react when Madoff was arrested and later confessed to running a Ponzi scheme? Clearly he did not fall on his sword, admit guilt or complicity in the crime. Nor did he work with the justice department or trustee to assist other investors.

"Mr. Chais is rightfully proud of his longstanding history of charitable giving and is saddened by the trustee's suit and outraged by the very public

way in which the trustee has proceeded, including suing Mr. Chais' children and their spouses and referring to Mr. Chais' grandchildren, none of whom had any decision-making involvement in the investments," Eugene Licker, attorney for Chais

It is not clear how much Chais invested of his own money nor have I uncovered information to estimate how much was raised through the Chais Funds. However, the trustee is suing Chais and other family members for $1 billion – the total of all withdrawals from 1995 forward.

Chais claims he knew nothing of the fraud!

Madoff paid for investor money

The above information detailing activities of a few who helped Madoff to fleece investors out of billions demonstrates the degree to which Madoff was willing to compensate his "co-conspirators and sales force." If you add the numbers up it is likely that this sales force actually received much more money out of the scheme than Madoff and his family.

Keep in mind that there are many, many more feeder funds than the few described in this chapter.

The following chart taken from my class shows the timing and size of the feeder funds discussed above.

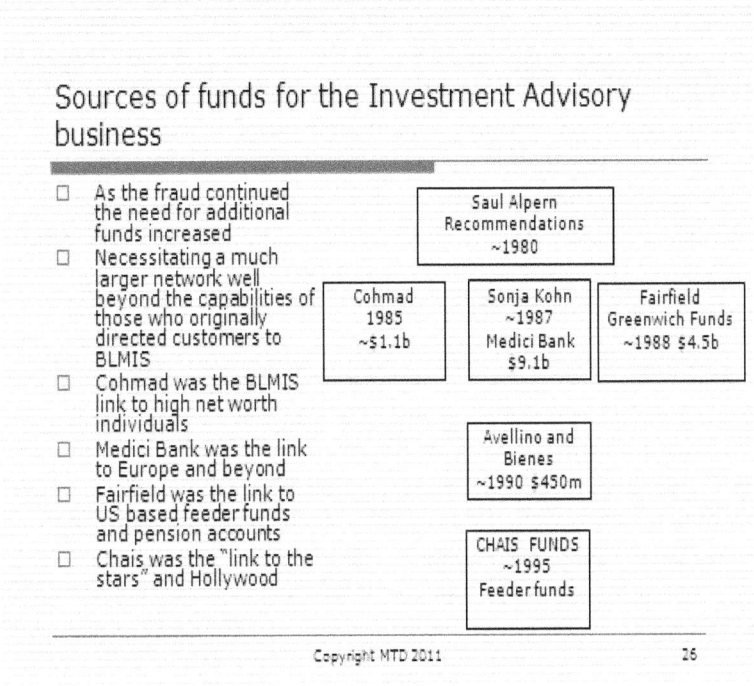

Sources of funds for the Investment Advisory business

☐ As the fraud continued the need for additional funds increased
☐ Necessitating a much larger network well beyond the capabilities of those who originally directed customers to BLMIS
☐ Cohmad was the BLMIS link to high net worth individuals
☐ Medici Bank was the link to Europe and beyond
☐ Fairfield was the link to US based feeder funds and pension accounts
☐ Chais was the "link to the stars" and Hollywood

Saul Alpern
Recommendations
~1980

| Cohmad 1985 ~$1.1b | Sonja Kohn ~1987 Medici Bank $9.1b | Fairfield Greenwich Funds ~1988 $4.5b |

Avellino and Bienes
~1990 $450m

CHAIS FUNDS
~1995
Feeder funds

Copyright MTD 2011 26

What about the banks

JPMorgan was Madoff's banker. The firm's account was the exclusive conduit for money coming in from investors as deposits, and money going out to investors as a result of redemption requests.

But JP Morgan was MORE than just the banker – the firm was also an investor. According to the SIPC trustee, in the later part of 2008, the bank had $276 million of its OWN money invested with Madoff. Apparently, executives became uncomfortable or suspicious with this investment because the firm withdrew $241 million shortly before Madoff was arrested.

JP Morgan also provided their customers with a means of investing with Madoff. Some "Madoff only" hedge funds provided JPMorgan with complex derivatives investment products that were sold to JPMorgan customers. By 2007,

JPMorgan sold $130 million of these products to their own customers. I do not know if JPMorgan informed these customers that the firm was withdrawing its own money while potentially leaving customers in a product they no longer trusted.

JPMorgan had information which should have made the firm suspicious. Since the firm had access to the flow of money into and out of the account, the very nature of the lack of any money used to purchase stocks should have raised many red flags.

If Madoff were running a REAL investment program there would have been transactions related to stock transactions. But Madoff was not trading anything; he was just printing paper, so there were no records of money going out to buy stocks or funds coming in as a result of stock sales. Was JPMorgan "looking the other way"; knowing that Madoff was running an investment advisory business was it not suspicious that there was no money transfers associated with trading activity? JPMorgan is also the target of litigation by the trustee.

> *"Defendants consistently wired funds to BLMIS' account at JPMorgan Chase & Co., Account # 0000001400081703"*

David J. Sheehan, an attorney for the SIPC trustee said that the Madoff scam "would not have been able to commit this massive Ponzi scheme without this bank."

JPMorgan claims they knew nothing of the scam!

6 THE PONZI SCHEME COLLAPSES

What does it take to make a Ponzi scheme function? The five point checklist shown below was executed to perfection by Madoff for many years.

- ☐ Constant inflow of new money
  - ■ Keep enough cash on hand to ensure there is enough to pay investor redemptions
- ☐ Build a network of co-conspirators to do the work of raising money and ensure their loyalty and silence with oversized compensation
  - ■ Madoff had a number of long-term employees and "fund raisers" who worked directly on operating and capitalizing the fraud
  - ■ Pay them well
- ☐ Portray the image of a real business
  - ■ BLMIS as a major Market Maker was a great cover
- ☐ Maintain an image of respectability
  - ■ Madoff had a sterling reputation in the industry
- ☐ Be absolutely ruthless and completely devoid of compassion
  - ■ Madoff was an equal opportunity thief.

> He took money from everyone;
> friends, neighbors, charities, pensions,
> widows, etc.

If Madoff was so good at it, why did the scheme fail?

Ponzi schemes collapse when the supply of new money dries up.

Madoff knew that without a continual supply of new investor money the scam would implode. Throughout the years Madoff needed to expand the web to ensnare more and more victims. He did not solicit this new money alone. Chapter 5 details just a few of the individuals that created feeder funds with the sole purpose of raising money for the IA business. Of course those operating these funds were very well compensated for their efforts. Madoff paid them so well they had no incentive or interest in stopping the fraud.

Madoff told investors they could request withdrawals from their account at any time. Easy access to funds was certain to create confidence amongst investors that their money was only a phone call away. If customers met with difficulties trying to make redemptions it just might raise questions causing them to withdraw even more – something Madoff must avoid!

What happens when many investors make redemption requests at the same time? Madoff would need a lot of money. To keep the scheme viable Madoff had to honor every single redemption. Madoff would be in a great deal of trouble if redemption requests exceeded money available in the bank to meet those requests. Failure to meet redemptions would lead to a "liquidity crisis" that must have terrified everyone involved in the scheme. Remember that redemptions could only be met by pulling new money into the scam or by borrowing money from some other source. I would think the "sales force" of feeder funds would be placed under great pressure to raise money quickly in the event Madoff faced redemptions he could not meet.

A liquidity crisis is the potential endgame of a Ponzi scheme. The flames in the burning building must be put out and the close call must be hidden from investors. Madoff did successfully navigate several earlier liquidity crisis events. It was the third incident in 2008 that led to Madoff's confession, subsequent guilty plea and 150 year prison sentence.

The liquidity crisis of 1992

The first "great escape" for Madoff occurred in 1992 when the SEC forced the closure of the Avellino and Bienes feeder fund.

A&B statements indicated client accounts were worth $450 million. A&B ostensibly kept all of that money at BLMIS and the SEC receiver ordered BLMIS to provide account records to substantiate the value of those accounts. Since Madoff was not actually trading anything the records did not exist making it necessary to "create" them. Madoff enlisted the help of a number of IA employees including DiPascali, Bongiorno, Crupi, and Bonventre to falsify the records requested by the SEC. And the SEC WAS fooled! Upon inspection of these records the SEC receiver ordered BLMIS to liquidate these fictional A&B positions and return the money to investors. The receiver inspected, but did not verify, ANY of the materials provided by Madoff thereby wasting a golden opportunity to end the scheme in 1992.

Of course, since there was no trading, there were no positions to liquidate and no money to pay off investors. In order to avoid discovery Madoff HAD to come up with over $400 million - and he had to do it very quickly. The trustee tells us how Bernard Madoff raised the money.

By 1992 Madoff had many wealthy non-split-strike clients along with a number of individuals running feeder funds. Both of these groups were making a lot of money and the collapse of the IA business would shut down the gravy train and start putting people in jail. Madoff went to two unnamed IA clients who provided real securities which Madoff then used as collateral to secure loans to pay off A&B investors. If the SEC investigators had any idea how Madoff raised the money the Ponzi scheme would have ended in 1992. But they never asked, and they never looked. Remember Ronald Regan's famous quote when dealing with the USSR "Trust But Verify"; SEC investigators did trust, but they NOT verify.

> "In order to provide funds for this purpose, in or about November 1992, Madoff obtained securities from at least two IA clients and used those securities as collateral for loans. Some of the loan proceeds were transferred to BLMIS bank accounts and were used to pay off a portion of the balance due the Receiver and, ultimately, A&B customers."

What Madoff giveth, Madoff taketh away! Madoff was forced to return money to investors. He borrowed that money from other investors whom I believe were quite aware of the fraud. Then he sent letters to people like me offering to open individual accounts with the "Master Trader" behind A&B. I believe he was able to get almost all of that money back – including mine!

The Liquidity crisis of 2005/2006

The 2nd liquidity crisis began in 2005 and ended in 2006. Madoff was saved again, but this time "the save" required crossing the financial bridge to the "legitimate" part of the business. To understand the "second great escape" it is important to understand the relationship between the N.Y. office (BLMIS) and the London office (MSIL).

THE MSIL LINK

Madoff Securities International Ltd., the London office of BLMIS is an important spoke in the wheel of crime. MSIL functioned more like a money laundering or money transfer facility to obliquely shift money from BLMIS to the IA business when needed.

In the early days before stocks were traded in decimals, the legitimate market-maker business was generating significant profits. On several occasions the IA business got into serious trouble with insufficient funds on hand to meet investor redemptions. Failing to meet a redemption request would lead to the demise of the scam. Money had to come in and come in very quickly. The legitimate, and profitable, market-making business was one source that could quickly be tapped. If discovered, it might seem odd and indefensible to just walk the check down from the 19th to the 17th floor. That is where MSIL comes in. Madoff could transfer money from BLMIS on the 19th floor, to London, and then back to the IA business on the 17th floor. **Abracadabra**, with a wave of the wire transfer magic wand, the redemption request would be honored.

As the margin between bid and ask narrowed from 1/8th to 1 cent the market-making business was much less profitable. The situation got so bad that the 19th floor was no longer self-supporting and needed a cash infusion of its own.

Indeed, the trustee suggests that without money transfers from the IA business the market-making business may have failed. To keep the 19th floor solvent, stolen IA money was transferred from the 17th floor, through London based MSIL, and then back to the 19th floor to support the "legitimate" business. If the legal business were to fail that might cause investigators to look too carefully at the operation two floors down. And that would be very bad. So the 19th floor business MUST have whatever assets were necessary to maintain operations. Although the funds should have been kept segregated, Madoff treated it all as one single pot of funds at his disposal for whatever needs he saw fit.

> "For fiscal year 2007, approximately $174 million dollars was transferred from the IA Business to an MSIL bank account. During this time period, approximately $103 million was transferred back to bank accounts controlled by BLMIS and appeared on the financial statements prepared for the market-making and proprietary trading businesses as commission income.
>
> For fiscal year 2008, approximately $90 million dollars was transferred from the IA Business to an MSIL bank account. During this time period, approximately $86 million was transferred back to bank accounts controlled by BLMIS and appeared on the financial statements prepared for the market-making and proprietary trading businesses as commission income.
>
> Based upon financial statements prepared by BLMIS for fiscal year 2007, this redirected commission income represented approximately 60% of the total revenues reported by the market-making and proprietary trading businesses. For fiscal year 2008, this re-directed commission

*income represented more than 70% of the
total revenues reported by the market-
making and proprietary trading
businesses.*

*The financial statements prepared by
BLMIS for fiscal years 2007 and 2008
falsely indicated that the market-making
and proprietary trading businesses
generated tens of millions of dollars in net
income. In reality, however, the market-
making and proprietary trading businesses
would have generated tens of millions of
dollars in losses had it not been
supported by the fraudulent transfer of
customer money, disguised as commission
income, from the IA Business."*

The following page from the class illustrates the flow of money
between several of the many feeder funds for the IA business
and Madoff's London and NY offices.   Money to support the IA
business came from a large number of sources including the
feeders listed below.   Money would go out to non-split-strike
clients as "returns" as well as providing compensation and
commission to employees and those running the funds.

The real key is to inspect the circular flow of money between
three BLMIS business entities.   The supply train would run in
different directions depending on which squeaky wheel needed
the oil.   If the IA business needed to meet customer
redemptions money would flow from the market-maker to the
IA business.   If the market-making business needed funds to pay
salary and bonuses the flow reverses from the IA business to the
market-maker business.

MSIL in London facilitated the fraud by masking the intent of these money transfers. One interesting point made during the class is to note the behavior of Mark and Andrew as money would suddenly "appear" from the London office to meet 19th floor operating expenses. They were running the 19th floor – were they not at all suspicious when hundreds of million inexplicably appeared in the business account! Madoff's two sons also saw the books for the operation and must have realized that without these transfers from MSIL the market-making business would have NO profits and the losses would have precluded payment of large salaries, bonuses and the "loans" that so many received from the firm.

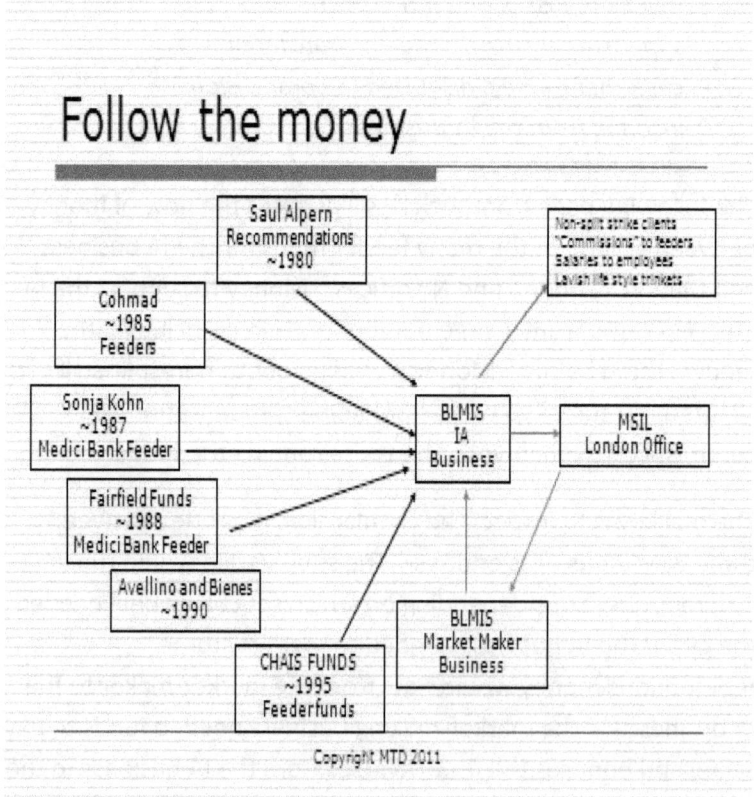

As we review the role of the SEC when investigating Madoff we will provide much more information about the role of MSIL in not only serving as a money transfer facility but also providing a cover to convince investigators both in the U.S. and Europe that he was actually trading.

We learn details about this 2nd liquidity crisis from the SEC complaint against the IA employee named Joanne Crupi. On November 2nd of 2005 Madoff was faced with $105 million in redemption requests. The IA bank account balance was $13 million – Madoff needed an additional $92 million. Just as in the 1992 event, Madoff needed to raise this money quickly – certainly within a few days. For unknown reasons Madoff did not go to other IA clients for the money this time. He simply transferred the money the next day from the 19th floor to the 17th floor using the London office as a conduit for the trade. This liquidity crisis was met using internal BLMIS assets. I wonder what the sons thought about $92 million disappearing from the operating account on the floor they managed?

There was little margin for error. The JPMorgan account showed a near zero balance. Any subsequent, near term redemption request would again generate a shortfall. And, a short time later, that is exactly what happened. I have to assume the 19th floor bank account balance was inadequate this time around since Madoff went to a "wealthy longtime investor" for a $100 million loan. This was provided in the form of government-backed securities which Madoff subsequently used as collateral for a bank loan. This was enough to put out the immediate fire.

But, it was not over yet. In January of 2006 Madoff borrowed an additional $50 million from the same investor to meet yet another round of investor redemptions.

*"On or about November 2, 2005, BLMIS's
Daily Report for the IA Bank Account showed
an end-of-day balance of approximately $13
million - a sum that was insufficient to cover
the approximately $105 million in payments
by BLMIS scheduled to be made to IA Clients
for the following three business days.*

*Therefore, funds were transferred from the
BLMIS Brokerage Accounts to meet the cash
needs of the IA operations on or about
November 3, 2005.*

*In the fall 2005, BMIS' suffered a liquidity
crisis. To survive this crisis, Madoff asked a
wealthy longtime investor for a loan. This
investor loaned BMIS $100 million in
government-backed securities in November
2005, which BMIS used as collateral for a loan
from a bank. The investor loaned Madoff an
additional $50 million in securities in January
2006, which Madoff used as collateral for
similar loan from the same bank. The
proceeds of the loan were deposited into the
Main Ponzi Scheme Account, and Crupi noted
this deposit in her daily report as a "BLM
special loan." These amounts were used
shortly thereafter to pay investor
redemptions totaling more than $300 million.*

*On or about January 18, 2006, IA Client A sent
another approximately $54 million. On or
about January 23, 2006, DANIEL BONVENTRE,
caused BLMIS to borrow another*

> *approximately $50 million using the Client A*
> *Bonds as collateral. The proceeds of the Client*
> *Collateralized Loans were deposited in the IA*
> *Bank Account and were used to satisfy*
> *requests for withdrawals from IA Clients."*

Things must have been getting pretty desperate in "Madoff land" during the first quarter of 2006. For the first time Madoff eschewed the safety of disguising money transfers by using the MSIL conduit and executed four wire transfers from the legitimate BLMIS Operating Account DIRECTLY to four separate IA clients. I wonder what the executives (Mark and Andrew) thought when they saw money from their operation going directly to Madoff's IA clients? The screen of plausible deniability provided by MSIL was gone!

> *"Between in or about January 2006 and in or*
> *about April 2006, deposits by IA Clients into the*
> *IA Bank Account failed to keep pace with*
> *requests for withdrawals by IA Clients*
>
> *Between in or about January 2006 and in or*
> *about April 2006, approximately four wire*
> *transfers totaling approximately $262 million*
> *were made from the BLMIS Operating Account*
> *directly to four separate IA Clients to satisfy*
> *their requests for withdrawals from their*
> *respective IA accounts"*

2005 and 2006 were tough years for Madoff's Ponzi scheme. You can only imagine the trauma in the office and the stress on everyone involved while working feverishly to prevent the collapse of the scandal. Of course, they were not trying to prevent the failure of a legitimate business; they were trying to continue the same criminal activity that had stolen investor money for decades and compensated them like royalty!

The trustee does not tell us if Madoff told the unnamed IA investor the purpose of the loan. Nor have I been able to ascertain whether this investor has been a target of any litigation by the trustee or justice department.

The Liquidity Crisis of 2008 – when the roof collapsed!

The 3rd liquidity crisis of 2008 proved to be "a bridge too far" and led directly to the inevitable unraveling of the entire Ponzi scheme.

The global financial crisis of 2008 was well underway and investors were pulling out of the stock market, housing market and pretty much selling any asset that might decline in value.

Madoff investors THOUGHT they were exposed to the fluctuations of the stock market and were especially wary of the potential for significant downward moves. In 2008 the stock market was proving to be a VERY scary place! Even though Madoff repeatedly proved to wield a deft hand in exiting the market and retreating to the safety of U.S. Treasuries whenever risk appeared, too many investors proved unwilling to remain exposed to securities.

Redemption requests skyrocketed!

By this point the Ponzi scheme reported investors were worth **$65 billion**. Clearly, the amount of money required to meet a significant number of redemptions would far surpass the funds that successfully resolved past liquidity events.

THE PROBLEM: The worldwide financial crisis of 2008 led to Madoffs' inability to meet large redemptions requested by investors.

THE SOLUTION: Could Madoff borrow enough to meet redemptions and preserve the viability of the Ponzi scheme?

By the fall of 2008, requests for redemptions made by IA Clients began to increase at a rate greater than investments made by new or existing clients.   Madoff's network of feeders was not raising enough cash fast enough to keep the wolves from the door.

By mid-November 2008, Bernard Madoff and the IA "Team" were concerned they would not be able to fulfill the requests for redemptions which were outpacing deposits at an ever increasing rate.

Once again the IA department entered crisis mode.   This was the third time around so they had a blueprint for how to handle the problem. But the sheer size of the redemption requests were larger than anything the firm had previously experienced. Past events solved with a loan or wire transfer of $100 million would prove woefully inadequate in 2008.

The numbers for cash-on-hand versus redemptions were sobering.   On November 3, 2008 the balance of the JPMorgan bank account reflected on the Daily Report (prepared by Crupi) showed a balance of approximately $487 million. Redemption requests totaled $1.447 billion, ten times what was available. The shortfall was ONE BILLION DOLLARS. Could Madoff again go to an "unnamed IA client" for something this big, or did he need to find a much bigger fish?

In early November, 2008 Madoff met with a billionaire investor named Ken Langone. Madoff's goal was to raise money by convincing Langone to invest in a brand new fund that Madoff was starting <u>only for new investors</u>. Langone apparently did not find the new fund sufficiently enticing – he declined the offer. I wonder what return Madoff promised Langone now that he was caught in a vise? Either it was not enough – or it was so high that it made the investor suspicious.

From November 2nd through November 20th new money did continue to come in and some redemptions were met. It was not enough.

On November 20, 2008, just a few days after the Langone rejection, an unnamed IA Client sent approximately $181 million of Federal Home Loan Bank ("FHLB") bonds to Madoff.   On November 25th these bonds were used to secure a loan and the IA Bank Account reflected a balance of $266 million.   Unfulfilled requests for redemptions totaled $759 million, a shortfall of $493 million.   But now the $181 million dollar loan was gone!

Date:	Cash on hand	Redemption Requests	**Shortfall**	Loans
November 3	$477m	$1,447m	**-$977m**	
November 20	$266m	$759m	**-$493m**	$181m

RATHER THAN ONE MORE "GREAT ESCAPE" MADOFF IA EMPLOYEES WERE FACING ARMAGEDDON!

WITHOUT NEW MONEY THE "GREAT COLLAPSE" WAS RIGHT AROUND THE CORNER.

CAN YOU JUST IMAGINE THE FRANTIC ACTIVITY AMONGST THOSE WHO WERE NOW FACING THE DISTINCT POSSIBILITY THAT THE PARTY WAS NEARLY OVER.

One December 1 and 2, 2008 additional funds in the amount of $181 million was transferred from the BLMIS Operating Account of the legitimate business DIRECTLY to the IA Bank Account. Again the safety and secrecy associated with using MSIL to transfer money was abandoned. Again, one must question what Mark and Andrew were thinking when this money disappeared into the rapidly deepening hole on the 17th floor.

Date:	Cash on hand	Redemption Requests	Shortfall	Loans/ Transfers
November 3	$477m	$1,447m	-$977m	
November 20	$266m	$759m	-$493m	$181m
December 4	$295m	$1,445m	-$1,150m	$181m

Things were rapidly falling apart. In spite of the best efforts of the "sales force", loans from unnamed IA clients and transfers from the legitimate business, on December 3, 2008 the net deficit to meet redemptions reached the princely total of **ONE BILLION, ONE HUNDRED AND FIFTY MILLION.** It was too much.

The rat was cornered!

"On or about December 3, 2008, JOANN CRUPI, a/k/a "Jodi," the defendant, and DiPascali met on a street corner near BLMIS. DiPascali told CRUPI that Madoff had just told him that BLMIS was out of money and that there were no assets standing behind the BLMIS obligations reflected in the IA Clients' account statements."

Preparing for the authorities

The trustee tells us the degree of desperation and the steps that IA employees were now taking to avoid the fallout from the upcoming nuclear explosion.

The following paragraph from the complaint seems like something you would read from the Watergate era. Imagine meeting on a street corner discussing what you are going to tell authorities and trying to devise a plausible reason for why you too were duped by the master criminal named Bernard Madoff.

> *"In the days following the December 3 meeting, JOANN CRUPI, a/k/a "Jodi," the defendant, and DiPascali discussed what they would say to law enforcement authorities once BLMIS eventually collapsed. DiPascali told CRUPI that he did not know what he would say. CRUPI told DiPascali that she was going to say that she thought that the trades executed on behalf of the IA Clients were being done overseas.*
>
> *On or about Sunday, December 7, 2008, JOANN CRUPI, a/k/a "Jodi," the defendant, and DiPascali met again in a restaurant in New Jersey and further discussed the liquidity crisis at BLMIS. CRUPI asked DiPascali what he was going to tell law enforcement authorities. CRUPI told DiPascali that she was "sticking to my story," and would tell law enforcement authorities that she thought that the trades executed on behalf of the IA Clients were being done overseas. CRUPI and DiPascali further discussed*

sending the remaining BLMIS funds to certain
LA Clients and employees."

The scam was collapsing. It was only a matter of time until the entire operation unraveled.

AMAZINGLY, IA EMPLOYEES CONTINUED TO TAKE NEW MONEY. AND THEY TRIED TO STEAL WHAT LITTLE WAS LEFT. FOR THESE CROOKS - IT WAS NEVER TOO LATE TO STEAL!

New money continued to flow into the IA coffers. Even though IA employees knew that the scam was over, they accepted $48 million of new deposits from investors in just the last few days before the bitter end.

> *"From approximately on or about December 3,*
> *2008, through approximately on or about*
> *December 10, 2008, Madoff, DiPascali, JOANN*
> *CRUPI, a/k/a "Jodi," the defendant, and others,*
> *continued to take in more than approximately*
> *$48 million of new deposits from investors."*

While new investors were depositing (and losing) their money, IA employees were preparing lists of preferred employees, family members and certain IA Clients (likely of the non-split-strike variety) who would be the recipients of the last millions left in the cupboard. The practice of stealing money had gotten so ingrained in IA employee behavior that they could not help themselves from directing the last remaining dollars toward their friends.

These "special" IA clients were to receive $300 million in checks in early December. Additional checks totaling $176 million were detailed in a journal entry on December 11th, the day that Madoff was arrested.

"During this time period, DiPascali, JOANN CRUPI, a/k/a "Jodi," the defendant, and others, prepared lists reflecting preferred employees, employee family members, and certain other IA Clients, and the balances in their respective IA accounts. DiPascali, CRUPI and others, also prepared checks, or caused checks to be prepared, for these preferred IA Clients so that the remaining BLMIS funds would be sent to them, thereby putting the interests of the select few IA Clients ahead of all of the other IA Clients. More than approximately $300 million in checks were prepared to be sent out to these preferred IA clients.

At the time BLMIS collapsed, JOANN CRUPI, a/k/a "Jodi," the defendant, had in her desk two Daily Journal Reports for December 11, 2008, listing the preferred IA Clients and the balances in their IA accounts, and reflecting CRUPI's handwritten calculations. CRUPI's desk also contained: a batch of checks made out to some of the preferred IA Clients in the amount of approximately $176 million; a Daily Journal Report for December 10, 2008, reflecting the amount of new deposits by IA Clients on that date; and several ripped up duplicate checks."

Time to face the music

I wonder why the entire crew of IA employees did not simply take the company plane and fly off to any country that did not have an extradition treaty with the U.S. Clearly the opportunity to run was available right up to the very end. And quite evidently, this group had few scruples that would prevent further illegal behavior like a flight to freedom from prosecution.

By December 10th the scheme collapsed. It was simply a case of waiting for the authorities to arrive with the handcuffs.

BUT, the authorities did not know anything about the Ponzi scheme. Somehow they had to be notified. This presented Madoff with a golden opportunity to protect his family and imply they were nothing more than innocent bystanders.

On the morning of December 10th, 2008 Bernard Madoff told his two sons the entire IA business "is one big lie." He asks his sons to wait one week before informing the authorities. I believe this was to give those last few checks time to clear. The trustee tells us the sons, on the advice of counsel, informed authorities later that day.

Bernard went home to tell his wife Ruth about the Ponzi scheme. Incredibly, the two of them then went to the office Christmas party.

The next morning at 10 a.m. the authorities, finally aware that a crime has been committed, arrive at Madoff's home, place him in handcuffs and take Bernard L. Madoff into custody.

7 THE "PLAYERS"; WHO DID WHAT? DID FAMILY MEMBERS KNOW

David Kugel ties together the legal activities on the 19th and the illegal operation on the 17th floors. His guilty plea tells us that the practice of using historical data to "report" trading activity originated on the 19th floor and these falsified trades were reported to customers of the IA business. But Kugel was only one person. Generating trade confirmations manually was slow and required too much manpower. How could the business possibly grow? Madoff needed either additional people to generate vastly more fake statements, or he would have to automate the process. Guess which one he chose?

A 97 page indictment filed in the US District Court, Southern District of NY names specific individuals and the process used to carry out the fraud. Below are the relevant players along with information about their role in the IA part of the business. Note that the name "David Kugel" is not listed in this section.

Technically he worked on the 19th floor and was involved during the early days before the process was automated to handle many more customers. It is also possible that investigators were not aware of the role of Kugel at the time the indictment was written.

There are a lot of capital letters showing financial industry positions, credentials and industry affiliations held by employees of the IA business. One would think that being named to such industry organizations would be a great honor. Only those who have been properly evaluated by their peers as being suitable to represent the industry need apply. Naming them to organizations tasked with regulating and overseeing the securities industry surely indicates that they are respected and trusted individuals held in high esteem by their colleagues.

You have to wonder how individuals involved in the biggest financial fraud in the history of the U.S. Securities industry got past the vetting process and sat on the very boards responsible for ensuring that fraud cannot occur in the brokerage business. In a situation analogous to hiring the fox to guard the henhouse, I often wonder if Madoff and his cronies were really that good at subterfuge, or if many in the industry were grossly negligent or simply willfully blind.

The definition of the letters and the powers, responsibilities and obligations of these organizations will be addressed in Volume II of this series.

- **■** Bernard Madoff
    - ☐ B.A. in political science with one year of law school
    - ☐ CEO and Chairman of BLMIS and majority shareholder of MLIS
- **■** Ruth Madoff (wife)
    - ☐ B.A. from Queens College in 1960
    - ☐ Served as bookkeeper responsible for account reconciliation of the IA business for more than 15 years
    - ☐ Controller at MSIL

- Peter Madoff (brother, employed 1965)
  - ☐ Attorney
  - ☐ Senior Managing Director and Chief Compliance Officer
  - ☐ Experienced investment professional holding at least 3 industry licenses and held several industry posts
    - Director of SIFMA
    - Member of the Board of Governors and Executive Committee of the National Stock Exchange
    - Vice Chairman of FINRA
    - Director of the National Securities Clearing Corp.
- Shana Madoff (Peter's daughter, employed 1995)
  - ☐ Attorney
  - ☐ Compliance Counsel, in-house Counsel, and Compliance Director of BLMIS and held a number of industry memberships
    - SIFMA Compliance and Legal Division Executive Committee
    - FINRA Consultative Committee
    - NASD's Market Regulation Committee
    - SIFMA Self- Regulatory and SRO Committee
    - SIFMA Continuing Education Committee
- Frank DiPascali (employed in late 1975)
  - ☐ Responsible for managing the thousands of the IA accounts using the "split strike conversion strategy

- **Daniel Bonventre (employed August 1968)**
  - ☐ Director of Operations
  - ☐ Responsible for all internal operations; maintaining and supervising the production of the internal accounting documents
  - ☐ Supervised the two programmers who wrote and maintained the IA software
- **Charles Weiner (Madoff's nephew)**
  - ☐ 30 year Madoff employee (1978)
  - ☐ Director of Administration
  - ☐ Worked on the 17th floor of the Lipstick Bldg
- **Annette Borgiorno (employed July 1968)**
  - ☐ Supervised employees who worked on IA business
  - ☐ Managed hundreds of IA accounts with a reported value of $8.5b
- **Joane Crupi (employed 1983)**
  - ☐ Tracked daily activity of the "703" bank account
  - ☐ Handled wire transfers into and out of the IA bank account
  - ☐ Assistant to DiPascali in managing split-strike conversion accounts
- **Jerome O-Hara (employed 1990) and George Perez (employed 1991)**
  - ☐ Developed and maintained computer programs that supported all three business operations; market making, Proprietary Trading and IA operations

We will address the alleged role of key individuals in the crime beginning with the two programmers.

Jerome O-Hara (employed 1990) and George Perez (employed 1991)

_Trading on the 19th floor was real. BLMIS used two computer systems to execute and report trading activity. One computer used the STRATUS trading platform, an industry standard that communicated with like systems at other companies to complete the buy and sell portions of real trades. STRATUS communicated this trading activity with an IBM AS/400 Server computer known internally at BLMIS as the "House 05" computer.

This IBM machine was the heart of the business in that it generated customer statements, internal and external reports and did much of the accounting for the firm. This machine also accomplished a very important industry requirement; it communicated every trade to a central reporting agency called the Depository Trust Company (DTC).

The DTC was created in 1973 as a means of making stock transactions more efficient. Prior to the DTC, brokers handled physical stock certificates and every transaction required processing these physical pieces of paper. DTC provided an electronic means of recording transactions, did away with physical certificates and made trading easier, faster and cheaper.

Actual trades executed by STRATUS and communicated to the House 05 computer included trade date, execution time, shares, stock symbols, etc. Since these were REAL trades it allowed those running the fraud to understand the exact process that occurred in a legitimate trading operation. If the appearance of that operation could be replicated in every detail then the criminal enterprise would meet all the specific visible requirement of a legitimate business. Of course, there is one part of the real business that a criminal would not want to replicate. Since trades were completely fictional - DO NOT report the trades to the DTC. The only persons told about the trades via their statements – were IA customers.

Madoff purchased an identical IBM AS/400 computer for the 17th floor. This was called the "House 17" computer. The STRATUS system was not needed because no trading actually transpired on the 17th floor. What was needed was a means of emulating the STRATUS system and sending what <u>appeared to be trade information</u> to the House 17 computer. Two programmers, Jerome O-Hara (employed 1990) and George Perez (employed 1991) did exactly that.

These two individuals wrote and maintained much of the software for both the House 05 and House 17 computers. Since they maintained the 19th floor computer operations for a real trading operation, they could take the identical software to the 17th floor. The programming to generate realistic trade confirmations and investor statements already existed from the 19th floor system. All they needed was a program to send fake trading data to the IA computer which would then generate fictional customer statements that looked like the real thing.

Madoff had now completed the feat that he described in a discussion about how fraud cannot occur in the securities industry. Bernie Madoff's own words on October 20th, 2007 tell us he actually accomplished this so-called impossible task. Madoff and the two programmers actually did program the computers to cheat – sometime around 1990, seventeen years BEFORE he tells us "we haven't gotten there yet."

> *"In today's regulatory environment it is virtually impossible to violate rules... It is impossible for a violation to go undetected, certainly not for a considerable period of time... so by taking the human being out of the equation to a great extent and turning it over to a computer to make*

a decision (laughter) – I guess you could always
program the computer to violate regulations
(laughter) but we haven't gotten there yet"

The two programmers were arrested by federal authorities on Friday, November 13, 2009 and charged with crimes associated with Madoff's Ponzi scheme.

How important were O-Hara and Perez? George S. Canellos, director of the Securities and Exchange Commission's New York Regional Office, said *"Without the help of O'Hara and Perez, the Madoff fraud would not have been possible."*

What would cause two men to work for an enterprise they almost certainly knew was a fraud? The same thing that drives so much reprehensible behavior on Wall Street – MONEY!

According to a federal criminal complaint against the two, Madoff gave orders to pay them *"whatever they wanted to keep them happy."* Comments made by Frank DiPascali, who also worked on the 19th floor and is under investigation, said Madoff ordered him to buy the silence of the two men. Both received $60,000 bonuses and 25 percent pay raises according to the complaint.

On March 25, 2010 Jerome O'Hara and George Perez pleaded not guilty in a Manhattan court.

Now all the parts of the puzzle were in place. Madoff has in place a legitimate business he can point to as an example of a successful firm which also serves to anoint the IA business with an aura of legitimacy. He has a copy-cat operation to replicate all the details of a real trading operation on the 17th floor. He has programmers to address any special software needs to both fake the business and generate reports to fool the regulators and customers. And he has a staff to process large amounts of fake trading volume. Now all he needs is lots of customer money.

Ruth Madoff provided access to a key component to starting BLMIS – a $50,000 loan from her father.

Ruth never acknowledged any role in the IA business nor did she admit knowing anything about it prior to Madoff's confession. The trustee indicated that Ruth worked as a bookkeeper for the IA business for approximately 15 years which suggests that the opportunity for "dirty hands" does exist.

Regardless of her degree of guilt Ruth did benefit from the success of the legitimate business operation of BLMIS as well as the revenue (note that I did not say profits) generated by the illegal IA business.

While Ruth professes her innocence, a review of how much money she withdrew from the business suggests an alternative interpretation of her behavior. I have not been able to find data prior to 2003, but Ruth withdrew almost $45 million from 2003 through 2008. More than half of that was withdrawn in just the last 2 years. From 2003 through 2006 the average annual withdrawal was just over $5 million a year while in 2007 and 2008 the average withdrawal more than doubled to almost $12 million annually. Why the dramatic increase in withdrawals?

Why would Ruth make these withdrawals from the illegal IA part of the business rather than the real business located on the 19th floor? I would also like a plausible explanation as to why Ruth would withdraw $11 million just 72 hours before Bernard was arrested - especially if she had no idea he was about to "confess to his sons" as she claims. I have been unable to find a single instance from 2003 through 2008 where Ruth made such a single large transfer. Finally, some portion of the $23 million withdrawn in the last 2 years came from accounts at MSIL (the London affiliate of BLMIS). Were the Madoffs also attempting to drain assets from this office before the great collapse?

1. Ruth made a total of 111 transfers from IA bank accounts during the period from 2003 through 2008 totaling $44,882,355
2. In the 2 years prior to Madoff's arrest, withdrew $23,765,534 from the IA bank account (funds withdrawn from both BLMIS and MSIL)
3. December 8th, 2008 (3 days before Madoff was arrested) withdrew $11m out of an IA account

Let's take a look at the assets the Madoff's accumulated from 1960 when Bernard founded BLMIS with $5,000 of his own money to 2008 when he was arrested for running a criminal enterprise while pretending to be a premier money manager.

Once BLMIS became a successful firm the Madoff's lived extravagantly and in every way maintained the appearance of the very wealthy. Some of the assets noted by the trustee include homes in Palm Beach FL, the south of France, the tip of Long Island, an ocean front home in New England and a $7 million penthouse in Manhattan. In addition to their real estate holdings the Madoff's had a private jet and three yachts appropriately named Sitting Bull, Little Bull and Little Maverick. The couple also owned millions in furniture to decorate their many homes and Ruth acquired expensive jewelry while Bernard had a Rolex watch collection.

Most, if not all, of this was purchased with money stolen from investors.

It is not surprising that Ruth was sued by the trustee considering the significant physical assets and recent large money transfers. After negotiations, Ruth agreed to surrender all family assets with the exception of $2.5 million in cash. Ruth worked a pretty sweet deal; I can think of many Madoff victims who would be tickled pink to walk away with that amount of cash.

Apparently normal rules of behavior, compassion for their victims and common decency do not apply to the Madoffs. "Steal what you can while you can" seems to aptly describe their behavior shortly after Madoff was arrested.

Ruth attempted to retain family ownership of her expensive jewelry in spite of a court order to preserve assets. The reckless and illegal behavior demonstrates the callousness of the couple and their total distain and disregard for those who trusted them. If Ruth was really "shocked" by the revelation of her husband's crime, the shocking and illegal attempted theft of remaining assets is difficult to understand and accept.

Just like Sonja Kohn who withdrew over $500 million from BLMIS right before the failure of the firm, Madoff and Ruth attempted to divert millions in assets just a few short weeks after Bernard was arrested. After Madoff was arrested on December 11th of 2008 he made bail and was confined to his luxurious NY penthouse apartment. Pending his confession and subsequent sentencing the Madoffs were ordered to safeguard all of their assets, disposing of absolutely nothing until the justice system determined rightful ownership. During Christmas of 2008, just a few weeks after his initial arrest, Bernard and Ruth packaged up several million dollars' worth of her jewelry and his Rolex collection mailing it to their sons. The sons, to their credit, contacted their attorney who alerted the justice department and the assets were confiscated. Several years later this jewelry, along with all other Madoff property, was sold and the proceeds will eventually be distributed to his innocent victims.

One final example of Bernard's total distain and contempt for his investors is demonstrated by his willingness to steal the few remaining cash assets of BLMIS at the same time that the whole scheme was falling apart. Bernard Madoff's Ponzi scheme was NEVER discovered by the regulatory authorities so these authorities were never able to swoop in and preserve what was left. Bernard "confessed" to his two sons, Mark and Andrew, on the afternoon of December 10th . Bernard asked his sons to wait a few days before turning him in to the authorities. There was a reason for asking for the delay. Authorities found checks in Madoff's desk in the amount of $173 million. These checks were made out to employees and favored investors. Madoff, even at the bitter end, was attempting to steal the last $173 million out of the $19 billion entrusted to his care ensuring that there would be absolutely nothing remaining for his victims.

After telling his sons that the entire IA business was "one big lie", Ruth, Bernard and their two sons met at the Manhattan penthouse. According to Ruth, she was "paralyzed" with shock upon being told that the business was a sham. Inexplicably, that night, just a few hours after being told that their entire world was to end, Bernard and Ruth attended a Christmas party at BLMIS. The next morning at 7 a.m. Bernard Madoff was arrested by the FBI.

My personal opinion is Madoff provided cover for his sons by giving them the opportunity to alert authorities to the scheme thereby casting doubt on their knowledge of, and involvement in, this crime. He further tried to insulate them from the crime by focusing their responsibilities on the legitimate 19th floor. Bernard gave his sons something we hear about all the time in politics – plausible deniability.

From my viewpoint, Bernard made a number of major mistakes when trying to provide cover for his sons and insinuate they were only innocent bystanders. **He paid and gave them too much money**. He gave them something called "loans" that he, and they, never expected to be repaid. He allowed them to open accounts with NO deposits and then reported millions in profits for those same zero based accounts. He put them on the board of London based MSIL and that office was an important cog for the illegal activities of the IA business.

A word about Madoff family members employed at BLMIS

The trustee tells us family members employed at BLMIS were highly educated, experienced in the financial industry and derelict in their duties at the firm.   Had any one of several family members been even slightly vigilant the entire scheme could have easily collapsed well before it grew to 65 billion dollars?

> *"The Family Defendants were, and frequently held themselves out to be, business and securities regulatory compliance managers and principals of BLMIS. The Family Defendants' management responsibilities extended through trading operations, customer relationships, and legal and regulatory compliance. Yet the Family Members were completely derelict in these duties and responsibilities. As a result, they either failed to detect or failed to stop the fraud, thereby enabling and facilitating the Ponzi scheme at BLMIS. Simply put, if the Family Members had been doing their jobs—honestly and faithfully— the Madoff Ponzi scheme might never have succeeded, or continued for so long."*

Perhaps there is a reason for keeping your head buried in the sand – money.   Persons with the surname "Madoff" working at BLMIS made a lot of it.   The Madoff family treated the business like their own personal piggy bank.   The trustee alleges family members benefited to the tune of more than $198 million from their association with BLMIS.   In just the last two years before the firm collapsed this group removed $58.7 million from the firm.   BLMIS was failing, Madoff was having a great deal of trouble raising new money to support the Ponzi scheme – and yet – family members just kept taking money out of the firm. Many successful investment managers entice clients into trusting them by making the claim "We treat your money like it was our own" – Madoff took those words very literally!

> "At this time, the Trustee has identified at least $198,743,299 of customer funds received by the Family Defendants. This amount, for the reasons set forth below, should be returned to the Trustee for the benefit of the customers of BLMIS. Included in this amount is $141,034,907 the Family Defendants received during the six-year period prior to Madoff's arrest and the demise of BLMIS on December 11, 2008. At least $58,666,811 of this amount is comprised of fraudulent transfers the Family Defendants received during the two-year period prior to December 11, 2008."

All have denied any knowledge of criminal activity at the firm. All were in a position to question the trading "profits" reported by Madoff and paid to them. All had the training and experience to seriously question whether any of the investment information provided by Madoff was real. If a mathematician was told that 2+2=5 he or she would KNOW that it was wrong. If an economist was told the US economy would grow by 5% in 2012 (not likely considering growth was under 2% the first half of the year) that economist would question the sanity of the person making the statement. Yet, family members willingly took incredible amounts of money out of the firm; ignoring the very real likelihood these investment gains were simply impossible to achieve without falsifying the data.

Now let's take a look at the positions held by Madoff family members, what they did and failed to do at the company, and how much money they were paid or took from the firm.

Peter Madoff (employed 1965)

Bernard's brother, Peter, held a law degree when hired in 1965 as one of the first employees at BLMIS.   Like others with the surname Madoff, Peter held a number of significant and prestigious positions in the securities industry including the following.

- Director of SIFMA
- Member of the Board of Governors and Executive Committee of the National Stock Exchange
- Vice Chairman of FINRA
- Director of the National Securities Clearing Corp.

Peter served as the Senior Managing Director and Chief Compliance Officer at BLMIS.   This is an important executive position at any securities industry.   The trustee tells us the person holding this position is responsible for overseeing activity at the firm to ensure that it complies with industry standards and meets its legal obligations.   This is the primary person responsible for identifying and preventing fraud at the company. So, why give this job to a family member: perhaps to ensure absolute silence and encourage a lack of vigilance. Why look the other way – because family members don't snitch and the compensation is enough to cause blindness to illegal activity.   Of course, it is also because they were in on it!

> "The Company's compliance and supervisory
> policies (and the laws and regulations mandating
> those policies) were supposed to insure that
> suspicious and irregular activity would be caught,

reported, and stopped. Instead, important compliance and supervisory roles were handed out to the Family Defendants who, rather than approach their jobs with appropriate professional diligence, failed to properly and faithfully carry out their duties and responsibilities."

Peter was one of the very few with key access to the IA business on the 17th floor. Considering that the Ponzi scheme ran under his watch for nearly 40 years one might conclude he was not very good at the job of Chief Compliance Officer. Either Peter was ineffective, incompetent or he was making and taking so much money that closing the scam down seemed like an extremely foolish decision. It is not that Peter did not have the proper industry training – he just chose not to use it at BLMIS.

Peter made money in three ways. First, he was paid a salary and bonus as an employee. Second, he had an IA account managed by his brother Bernard. Third, he took out a number of loans from the company – which the firm graciously never forced Peter to repay.

As an employee Peter was paid $20,067,920 in salary and bonus for the eight year period from 2001 through the collapse in 2008 – an average of $2.5 million per year.

Peter actually had two IA accounts. But these were a little different from my account – he put in a lot less of his own money, and his accounts earned a lot more.

I have not been able to discover when these accounts were opened, but the trustee determined that Peter deposited a total of $32,146 only fourteen dollars of which was invested after December 1995. Over the years Peter *withdrew* $16,252,004 or *five hundred and six times* more than he invested. What a sweet deal! The economist who was told the US economy would grow by 5% would be flabbergasted – and I suspect that any legitimate investment professional would be rightfully suspicious of such numbers.

One of the accounts (#1M0174) was never funded at all. Yet the March 2002 statement shows a transaction in Microsoft stock that generated a "gain" of $8,752,620. Amazingly - an account that had no deposits showing profits of $8.8 million. Would anyone believe these numbers? **Peter did!**

> *"Notwithstanding the lack of actual investment, the March 2002 account statement reflects transactions in Microsoft stock generating a purported gain of $8,752,620. These trades were a complete fabrication. Despite having no money or securities invested in the account, Peter's investment account suddenly shows that approximately $15.4 million worth of Microsoft stock had been "purchased" in or about December 2000 and "sold" in or about January 2002. The first evidence of this "purchase" of Microsoft stock does not appear until March 2002. Less than two months later, on or about May 17, 2002, Peter Madoff redeemed nearly $6 million from this account, which included the gains from the fabricated Microsoft transactions. The purchase and sale of Microsoft shares reflected on Peter Madoff's account statements were a complete fiction. They never occurred. They were simply typed out on his account statements to justify his withdrawal of nearly $6 million of other people's money."*

The trustee tells us Peter's account was treated in the same fashion as other preferred customer non-split-strike accounts. Statements received by Peter show backdated trades and buys and sells in accounts with no trading balance: *"There were a number of backdated trades, and "buys" of securities where there were no funds available for purchase."*

Peter was an investment professional. He must have known that backdated statements were a real no-no. He must have known that making millions from nothing was impossible in the real world. Working at a securities firm he should have known that the returns he was getting were ridiculous. His job title mandated that he look for, recognize and report fraudulent activity. He did NONE of this! Peter did not suffer from this deaf, dumb and blind behavior – Madoff's other investors did.

> *"Consistent with his level of financial experience and sophistication and his role as CCO, defendant Peter Madoff knew, or should have known, that the amounts withdrawn from his accounts were the product of fictitious and backdated trading activity and that the benefit he received was derived from purported transactions grounded in fraud and deception. He ignored obvious red flags that the profits reflected in account statements could not have been earned legitimately, to the detriment of BLMIS and its other customers."*

Let's take a look at Peter's third source of income – loans, advances or some other fabricated pretext used to transfer about $20.6 million of IA investor money to Peter Madoff. A review of the complaint filed by the trustee shows the nature of these monetary transfers. We have low interest "loans"; purchase of a NY apartment; purchase of a FL home; premium for a life insurance policy; buying shares in businesses, restoring an antique automobile and paying personal expenses on an American Express card. All these benefits, and a salary too – does it get any better than this!

> *"On December 12, 2007, Bernard Madoff "loaned" Peter $9,000,000 at a low interest rate of 4.13%. Although the note was payable to Madoff, personally, the money for the loan came from the operating account for BLMIS's IA Business at JP Morgan Chase Bank (the "703 Account"). Despite the favorable terms, the Trustee has not discovered any evidence that interest or principal has been paid on this loan;*

> *.On April 14 and June 2, 2004, $4.45 million was wired from the 703 Account to Peter in connection with the purchase of an apartment located at 975 Park Avenue, Apt. 6B, New York, NY;*

> *In April of 2001, Peter's sister-in-law, Ruth Madoff, "loaned" him $4,244,649.30 in connection with the purchase of a home located at 200 NW Algoma Road, Palm Beach, FL 33480. That money, however, was wired directly to Peter's real estate agents and lawyers from various BLMIS operating accounts;*

> *.Between 1996 and 2008, BLMIS paid $1,016,622 (in 38 separate payments) from its account at the Bank of New York to the Peter B. Madoff Life Insurance Trust, funding*

a life insurance policy which named his family members as beneficiaries;

Peter was also an investor in four limited partnerships operated by Sterling American Property, Inc. (the "Sterling Partnerships"). Between January 18, 2000 and April 11, 2006, the Sterling Partnerships received twelve payments totaling at least $896,744 from BLMIS on Peter's behalf;

Peter held a 1% ownership stake in Madoff Brokerage Trading and Technology, LLC, which was financed by a $35,000 payment from one of BLMIS's operating accounts;

Peter also held a 1% ownership stake in Madoff Technologies, LLC. On October 31, 2000, his portion of a capital call by that entity—$54,915.25—was paid by a transfer from one of BLMIS's operating accounts;

MSIL paid approximately $274,562 out of its operating account (in four separate payments) for the purchase and restoration of Peter's Aston Martin automobile;

Between 2002 and 2008, BLMIS funds were used to pay for $747,046 in personal expenses charged to Peter's American Express cards for personal expenses such as, for example, wines and luxury clothing"

None of these "loans" were ever repaid.

On Friday, June 29th, 2012 Peter Madoff appeared in a NY courthouse and pleaded guilty to several charges. He will remain free until his sentencing on October 4th. What kind of a deal was Peter able to wrangle from authorities, what did he admit, and how will he be punished?

Peter pleaded guilty to the following.

1. Faking documents
2. Lying to regulators
3. Filing false tax returns

None of these included admitting he knew anything about the Ponzi scheme prior to December 2008. But Peter did admit that between the time he learned of the fraud and Bernard's arrest, the two brothers tried to divert the remaining funds to Madoff's friends and family (remember the $173 million in checks found in Madoff's desk by authorities the morning of his arrest). During the court appearance Peter said *"I am deeply ashamed of my actions. I want to apologize to anyone who was harmed."* I question the sincerity of his apology – especially since he, along with Bernard, was trying to steal the last of the loot before the roof caved in! **By the time of this latest theft – there was NO QUESTION that Peter knew it was all a fraud. He tried to steal the money anyway!**

As part of the plea arrangement Peter agreed to serve at least 10 years in prison. He also agreed to forfeit $143.1 billion. Obviously this will never be paid. $143.1 billion is the trustee's estimate of the amount that went through IA accounts during the time Peter worked at the firm.

Shana Madoff (employed 1995)

Peter's daughter, Shana, held a law degree when hired in 1995. By this point the fraud was well underway with money coming in from feeder funds such as Chais, Cohmad, Bank Medici and others. Like her father and other Madoff's, Shana too held a number of positions in the securities industry including the following.

- SIFMA Compliance and Legal Division Executive Committee
- FINRA Consultative Committee
- NASD's Market Regulation Committee
- SIFMA Self- Regulatory and SRO Committee
- SIFMA Continuing Education Committee

Shana's title at the firm was "Compliance Counsel, in-house Counsel, and Compliance Director of BLMIS." The words "compliance" and "counsel" appear four times in the title demonstrating that Shana, like her father, had responsibility to oversee activity at the firm to ensure compliance with rules, regulations and laws. And like her father, she failed to discover any anomalies at the firm.

To understand this benign neglect we once again need to "follow the money."

Shana received $3,832,878 in salary and bonus between 2001 and 2008, an average of $479,110 annually.

Like every other Madoff, Shana deposited money into the IA business. In fact, she had five accounts in her own name and that of her family members. The Trustee reports that Shana deposited $1,364,975 into those accounts. Prior to the collapse of BLMIS Shana redeemed $1,666,436. Unlike her father whose account value increased over 500 times, Shana showed a rather poor return of only $301,461. I have not been able to determine the value shown on her last account statement so the reported rate of return cannot be estimated.

Lest you feel too sorry for the relatively poor results of Shana's IA accounts I feel compelled to point out another source of revenue for Shana – loans, or gifts or advances or whatever else you would call a transfer of $6,477,353.71.

Note the text from the trustee complaint shown below. BLMIS money (stolen from IA investors) was used to buy a home, buy shares in other Madoff businesses, decorate the home paid for with IA money, pay rent and pay off an American Express credit card. What an AMAZING job – the riches just keep on coming!

> *"On March 28 and May 8, 2008, a total of $2,899,000 million, originating from the 703 Account, was used to purchase Shana a home at 8 Barclay Court, East Hampton, NY 11937*
>
> *Shana held a 22.275% interest in Madoff Technologies, LLC. On October 31, 2000, a capital call to that entity was satisfied by a payment from BLMIS's operating account, $1,223,237.19 of which was attributable to Shana's ownership stake;*
>
> *On or about July 2, 2007, Shana purchased a one-third stake in Madoff Energy Holdings, LLC for $2,370,000. $1,700,000 of that amount, however, was taken from various BLMIS operating accounts and recorded as a purported draw against her father, Peter Madoff's, compensation;*
>
> *In September and October of 2000, $30,000 was sent from BLMIS's operating account at the Bank of*

New York to Shana's interior decorator;

*Between 2002 and 2004, BLMIS paid $241,958 to
the Gleenwood Management Corporation for rent
on Shana's apartment*

*Between 2002 and 2008, BLMIS funds were used
to pay for $379,342 in personal expenses charged to
Shana's American Express card such as clothing,
cosmetics, and personal travel."*

Shana, like so many others who profess their innocence and
claim to have been duped by Bernard Madoff, had an inside
track on observing what was happening in the IA business. She
worked there for 13 years. She was tasked with the job of
overseeing compliance with securities laws. She sat on
industry committees that interpreted and enforced industry
regulations. Shana undoubtedly worked on BLMIS filings for the
SEC. What are we talking about here – negligence, stupidity or
benign neglect? Did she deliberately ignore red flags indicating
fraud or was she too incompetent to recognize them!

One last intriguing tidbit about Shana involves her marriage to
an SEC enforcement lawyer named Eric Swanson. Mr. Swanson
worked at an SEC office that performed one of the multiple
investigations of BLMIS. The SEC has determined that the
marriage of Shana to an SEC enforcement office had nothing to
do with the Madoff fraud. It just seems a little odd to me that
Shana was responsible for complying with SEC regulations at
BLMIS, was married to an SEC enforcement official whose office
investigated BLMIS, and there was nothing problematic about
any of this.

At this point in time, Shana has not been charged with any
criminal activity. She is being sued by the trustee. She now goes

by her married name of Swanson, rather than Madoff.

Mark Madoff (employed 1986) and Andrew Madoff (employed 1988)

Bernard's college educated sons joined the firm in the late 1980's. This was before the programming was completed by Jerome O'Hara and George Perez which replicated the process of real trading activity occurring on the 19th floor. At this time, David Kugel would necessarily be very active in manually falsifying trade tickets for IA customers. Remember that Kugel worked on the 19th floor; therefore he worked **for the sons who claim they knew nothing of what he was doing.**

The two sons did not work on the 17th floor where Bernard ran the IA business. Rather the father had the sons run the market-making and proprietary trading operations on the 19th floor.

Why keep the sons out of direct contact with the IA business? Perhaps to create an opportunity for plausible deniability allowing the sons to disavow any knowledge of the Ponzi scheme; perhaps Bernard really planned to deceive his sons by isolating them from the crime being committed two floors below. Regardless of the reason for directly separating them from the IA operations, the father did bring his sons into a business **he knew** would eventually fail bringing the wrath of the justice department on everyone directly or indirectly connected to the venture.

Like every Madoff, these two highly educated and experienced individuals held prestigious industry posts. Volume II of this book series will discuss how important these organizations are to the securities industry and the honor associated with sitting on these committees. As FINRA registered principals of a securities firm, both Mark and Andrew had the responsibility to ensure that the firm's policies and procedures were in compliance with industry regulations and securities laws.

- **Mark Madoff (employed by BLMIS in 1986)**
  - ☐ University of Michigan graduate
  - ☐ Held at least 3 industry licenses
  - ☐ Held many industry positions
    - Chairman of the FINRA Inter-Market Committee
    - Governor of the Securities Traders Association
    - Co-Chair of the STA Trading Committee
    - Member of FINRA Membership Committee and Mutual Fund Task Force
    - President of the STA of New York
    - Chairman of the FINRA Regulation District Ten Business Conduct Committee
    - Chairman of the SIFMA NASDAQ Committee

- **Andrew Madoff (employed by BLMIS in 1988)**
  - ☐ University of Pennsylvania Wharton Business School graduate
  - ☐ Held at least 4 industry licenses
  - ☐ Held two industry positions
    - Chairman of the Trading, Trading Issues and Technology, and Decimalization and Market Data Committees and Subcommittees at SIFMA
    - Member of the FINRA District Ten Committee and NASDAQ's Technology Advisory Committee

The job titles for Mark and Andrew are indicative of significant positions at the firm. Both shared the title of "Co-Director of Trading at BLMIS" – they ran the proprietary trading department for the firm.   I have not been able to discover any documentation as to the trading performance of this activity. One has to wonder how successfully the sons traded versus the performance of the IA department two floors below.

A seasoned professional running a trading desk would know the particulars of a real trading operation and the range of achievable and believable returns.   The sons were seasoned and they tell us they were trading professionals. Each worked at the firm for 20 years as a director of trading. Any significant variation from the norm would be certain to raise red flags for an investment professional.   Returns outside the range can only mean two things - either the money manager is really good – or he is a fraud! The sons should have been able to tell the difference. Like Peter Madoff, they too chose to look the other way and take the money.

Life must have been SO, SO good – great job, wonderful reputation, the respect of your colleagues, positions on powerful industry committees and enough money to live well beyond the top 1% we so often hear about in political discussions around election time.

One again "follow the money" to understand how behavior tells a different story than words.

Mark Madoff – compensation and payments

Mark led a life in line with the reputation of being the son of a wealthy Wall Street icon. He was also a highly compensated firm executive. But just how high is up and how much should you pay an executive at a broker-dealer firm. The news indicates that compensation is virtually unbounded and executives are routinely paid in the millions or even tens of millions. But these executives are paid out of firm profits. By the early 2000's it is questionable if BLMIS had any real profits at all. What the firm did have was IA investor money coming in. Bernard Madoff determined that this could be used to compensate employees in the broker-dealer department whenever revenue fell short of expectations.

So let's review Mark's monetary take which comes in two flavors; salary and return from his IA accounts managed by Bernard on the 17th floor.

Mark received a salary from 2001 to 2008 totaling $29,320,830 or an average of $3.7 million a year. After the firms' collapse Mark filed for an additional $44,815,520 in deferred compensation. This has been denied by the trustee.

> "The Trustee has thus far identified a total of at least $66,859,311 that Mark Madoff received improperly from BLMIS. Mark Madoff lived a high-end lifestyle with homes in Manhattan, Nantucket, and Greenwich, Connecticut. BLMIS funds paid for all aspects of his lavish lifestyle from the purchases of his high-end homes to the mattress and box spring he slept on, the television he watched in his home gym, and the outdoor shower in his home. In addition, BLMIS provided Mark Madoff with astronomical compensation— between 2001 and 2008, he was paid $29,320,830, including bonuses of $4.8 million in 2006 and over $9 million in 2007."

Mark's IA accounts were similar to mine in name only. Similar to the mystical performance of Peter Madoff's accounts which made something out of nothing, Mark's accounts also showed millions in profits. Mark had seven IA accounts. He deposited a total of $745,482 and withdrew $18,105,456, twenty-four times his original investment. If indeed Mark considered this return real, then why would he continue to run a proprietary trading desk on the 19th floor where the rate of return was likely only a tiny fraction of what his father was able to accomplish!

> *"Among other accounts, Mark maintained seven customer accounts with the IA Business for himself and his family members. The Trustee has identified documents purporting to show that Mark invested a total of $745,482 into those accounts. Nonetheless, Mark was able to redeem $18,105,456 from his investment accounts prior to December 2008. It was—or at the very least, should have been—obvious to Mark that the massive gains reflected in his customer account statements did not reflect actual securities transactions or market conditions."*

Account number 1M0142 was never funded by Mark. Yet he was about to make substantial withdrawals as profits to the tune of $14,607,966 miraculously appeared in the account. Our mathematician would be both amazed and amused that you could take ZERO dollars in, and apply any rate of return that would generate a $14.6 million profit.

> *"One of these accounts—1M0142—was purportedly opened in July 1998. Although the Trustee has not found any record of money invested into that account, Mark redeemed $14,607,966 from that account alone."*

Finally, we cannot forget one of the other distinguishable

characteristics of non-split-strike accounts in the never-never land of Madoff. Backdated trades were also part of the process and one of the key benefits of these accounts. This account is unique in the extensive degree of backdating – trades occurred 18 months BEFORE the account was opened.

> *"Mark Madoff received millions of dollars as a result of fictitious and backdated transactions in his IA account. In July 1998, almost immediately after the account was opened, the account statement purported to show that thousands of shares of Dell Computer Corporation ("Dell") stock had been purchased in or about January 1997, <u>more than eighteen months before the account was opened</u>."*

Like every other Madoff, we cannot neglect to mention the pattern of "loans" received as additional compensation. This compensation is really nothing more than a different (and possibly non-taxable) means of transferring IA investor money to the Madoff clan. Mark's haul totaled $20,178,507 or almost 68% of the taxable salary he received from BLMIS. Like every other Madoff these loans were used for homes, purchase of other businesses and payment of personal expenses charged to an American Express card. And like every other loan to the Madoffs, these loans were never repaid. When you look at the size and scope of these loans you just have to ask yourself the question "what were these guys thinking?" How could they possibly close their eyes and be so ignorant of the relevance of the money flowing to them and not question the source of this seemingly endless bounty of riches.

"In May and June of 2008, $6,645,000 was transferred from the 703 Account directly to Mark's real estate attorney for the purchase of a home located at 51 Wanoma Way, Nantucket, MA 02554. Although this transfer took the form of a purported "loan" with a 3.2% interest rate, the Trustee has found no evidence that this loan was ever serviced or that any amount was repaid to BLMIS;

In June 2005, Mark's mother, Ruth Madoff, purported to loan him $5,556,589 in connection with the purchase of an apartment located at 583 Broadway, Apt. 4M, New York, NY 10021. Those funds, however, originated from the 703 Account. The Trustee has found no evidence that this loan was ever serviced or that any amount was repaid.

In February 2001, BLMIS sent four checks from its operating accounts totaling $1,232,680 to fund Mark's purchase of an apartment on Manhattan's Upper East Side;

In 2000, Mark purchased a $2,242,500 home located at 21 Cherry Valley Road, Greenwich, CT 06831. On information and belief, this amount was funded directly from BLMIS's operating accounts. Again, some of these payments were documented as a purported "loan" from his mother, however the Trustee has found no evidence that such a loan was ever serviced or the amounts repaid to BLMIS;

Mark held a 22.275% ownership stake in Madoff Brokerage Trading and Technology, LLC, which was financed by a $779,625 payment from one of

BLMIS's operating accounts;

*BLMIS funds were used to pay for $797,113 in
personal expenses charged to Mark's American
Express card between 2002 and 2008.*

*Only a year earlier, in March 2004, Mark's
mother had purported to loan him $2,925,000 to
purchase another Manhattan apartment. Once
again, however, the money originated from the 703
Account, and the "loan" was never serviced or
repaid;"*

On December 11th, 2010 two years after his father's
arrest Mark committed suicide by hanging himself
with a dog leash in his N.Y. apartment while his 2
year old son slept in another room. Just one more
tragic event traceable directly to the Ponzi scheme
started by his father decades ago.

Andrew Madoff – compensation and payments

As I read through complaint after complaint filed by
the trustee, my amazement continued to grow at the
guile of the Madoffs as they continued to accept
increasingly large payments that came from IA investor
deposits. Even as the business was failing in 2007 and
2008 the payments continued at record rates.   I am
not sure if the recipients of this great largess thought
the gravy train would never stop, of if they decided
that one last money grab would simply not matter
since the end was near.

The story of the mixture of salary, IA account
performance and loans for Andrew is similar to that of

Mark and Peter. It appears that Bernard treated the two brothers about equally. That means Bernard was perfectly willing to give each of them an equal share of someone else's money.

Andrew received $31,105,505 in salary from 2001 to 2008 or an average of $3.8 million per year. For some unknown reason Bernard paid Andrew slightly more than his brother. The bonus of $9 million in 2007 was more than three times the average paid in prior years supporting the observation that theft increased as the business withered.

Andrew claimed he was owed additional deferred compensation in the amount of $40,624,525. This claim was denied by the trustee. I guess the amount of the claim for deferred compensation is dependent on who is reading the claim. When addressing BLMIS the claim was for $40 million; when Andrew filed divorce papers where his ex-wife would claim her share of this compensation, the stated claim was reduced to $52,173. Just one more lie to authorities – no big deal!

> *"Like his brother, Andrew Madoff also lived a high-end lifestyle funded by the investment funds entrusted to BLMIS by its customers. The Trustee has thus far discovered $60,644,821 transferred from BLMIS to Andrew Madoff or to entities on his behalf. Between 2001 and 2008, Andrew was paid $31,105,505 in salary and bonus. His compensation included bonuses of over $4.8 million in 2006, and over $9 million in 2007, alone. Beyond this amount, in a proof of claim*

filed with this Court, Andrew seeks an additional $40,624,525 in deferred compensation. Although the Trustee has discovered self-serving documents, created by Andrew, stating that he is owed over $9.5 million in deferred compensation as of March 2008, there is no evidence that anywhere near this level of compensation was, in fact, deferred.

At any rate, in documents filed in connection with Andrew's divorce proceeding, he disclosed that his unpaid deferred compensation was only $52,173. On information and belief, these compensation amounts, if any, were based on or composed of the false profits reported in the Company's IA Business and the monies of other BLMIS customers, and are avoidable by the Trustee."

Andrew also had seven IA accounts. These too were of the non-split-strike variety meaning they benefited by accruing profits without funding, backdated trades and whopping returns. Andrew deposited $912,062 and redeemed $17,117,566 or nearly nineteen times his original investment.

Account number 1M0140 showed redemptions of $14.5 million — all without the benefit of a single penny ever being deposited into the account.

As in Mark's case, this account reported trading activity 18 months prior to being opened.

> *"Among other accounts, Andrew maintained seven investment accounts in his name. The Trustee has learned so far that Andrew invested $912,062 into those accounts, yet was able to redeem $17,117,566 prior to December 2008. It was—or at the very least, should have been—obvious to Andrew that the gains reflected in his customer account statements did not reflect actual securities transactions or market conditions.*
>
> *Most, but not all, of Andrew's IA account gains were withdrawn from customer account number 1M0140. Although the Trustee has not found that any money was invested into this account, over $14.5 million was redeemed between 1998 and November 2008.*
>
> *The purported profits generated by this customer account were the result of brazenly fabricated transactions. In July 1998, almost immediately after the account was opened, the account statement purported to show that thousands of shares of Dell Computer Corporation stock had been purchased in or about January 1997, more than eighteen months before the account was opened. These purchases occurred even though the account was never funded with cash or securities."*

Lest we forget: Andrew also benefitted financially from BLMIS loans in the amount of $13,322,812. As in the case of every other employee with the name Madoff, these loans were used for homes, purchase of businesses and American Express payments for personal expenses. Unlike other Madoff's, stolen investor IA money was also used for boats, fly fishing equipment and a hunting membership for Andrew. Clearly, he was an active sportsman – he just wanted someone else to pay for it!

"In 2008, Bernard Madoff purported to "loan" Andrew $4,485,000 for the purchase of an apartment located at 433 E. 74th Street, Apt. 5E, New York, NY 10021. That money, however, was wired directly to Andrew's real estate agents and lawyers from the 703 Account. The Trustee has not discovered any evidence that this "loan" was ever serviced or repaid;

.On November 25, 2003, Ruth Madoff purported to "loan" Andrew $6.8 million to purchase another apartment located at 10 Gracie Square, Apt. 10G, New York, NY. That money, however, originated from the 703 Account and the Trustee has not found any evidence that this "loan" was ever serviced or repaid;

.Andrew held a 22.275% ownership stake in Madoff Brokerage Trading and Technology, LLC, which was financed by a $779,625 payment from one of BLMIS's operating accounts;

Andrew's $300,000 interest in a business called Blow Styling Salon, LLC was funded with transfers from the 703 Account in May and September of 2008;

.In 2003, the $12,000 down payment on Andrew's boat was paid with a check issued by one of the BLMIS operating accounts;

.In 2002, BLMIS paid $68,900 to the Beacon Point Marine in Connecticut where, on information and belief, Andrew kept the boat paid for, in part, by BLMIS;

.In 2001 and 2002, BLMIS funds were used to pay $75,000 to "Lock and Hackle," a fly fishing and hunting membership club in Miami, Florida on Andrew's behalf;

.Between 2002 and 2008, BLMIS funds were used to pay for $813,287 in personal expenses charged to Andrew's American Express card such as clothes, boat rentals, and vacation travel for his wife and daughters."

Andrew continues to deny any prior knowledge of the Ponzi scheme. Andrew has not yet faced criminal charges by the justice department, but he, along with other Madoff family members, is the target of a financial claim by the trustee.

Although most assets were frozen, Andrew apparently has access to other funds. In early June of 2012, Catherine Hooper, Andrew's fiancée, tried to rent a NY apartment. The application was denied once she listed the name of her fiancée on the agreement. Of course, everyone has to live somewhere - but the monthly rental fee of $20,000 shows that the cupboard was not yet bare and Andrew retained access to large amounts of money. I know it is NY, but still – for $20,000 a MONTH this must have been pretty nice digs – much better than many of the victims of this scheme are able to afford.

Michael T. De Vita

Two tables from the class show a summary of "the Madoff family take."

The numbers for their IA accounts are nothing short of astounding:

Money In: $3,054,665

Money Out: $53,141,462

Madoff family members received gains of FIFTY MILLION dollars on an investment of THREE MILLION.   Only in the make believe world of the Madoff IA business is that possible – and it is should NEVER have been believable – unless of course – **THEY ALL KNEW!**

	Madoff Family Member IA Account Performance		
	Money In	Money Out	Gains
Mark	$745,482	$18,105,456	$17,359,974
Andrew	$912,062	$17,117,566	$16,205,504
Peter	$32,146	$16,252,004	$16,219,858
Shana	$1,364,975	$1,666,436	$301,461
Total	$3,054,665	$53,141,462	$50,086,797

Of course, the IA accounts were not the only source of funds. Salaries, bonuses, cash withdrawals and gratituous "loans" were also available to those with the surname Madoff. Note that the list now include Ruth's withdrawls from BLMIS accounts. I was only able to get data for the years 2001 through 2008 meaning that the Madoff clan received far more money than what is reported in this table.

	Madoff Family Member "Other" Income		
	Salary/ bonuses/ cash	Loans	
Ruth	$44,882,355		2003-2008
Mark	$29,320,830	$20,000,000	2001-2008
Andrew	$31,105,505	$13,000,000	2001-2008
Peter	$20,067,920	$20,000,000	2001-2008
Shana	$3,532,578	$6,000,000	2001-2008
Total	$128,909,188	$59,000,000	

8 DECEMBER 20, 2012 – SENTENCING HEARING FOR PETER MADOFF

The initial sentencing hearing for Peter Madoff was scheduled for October 4th of 2012. That hearing date was postponed. Early in December the U.S. Attorney notified many victims that the hearing was rescheduled for December 20th. As in the Bernard Madoff sentencing hearing on June 29th of 2009, victims were again invited to attend, to write victim impact statements, and to speak at the hearing.

A call to Wendy Olsen, who worked for the U.S. Attorney Office in NY, indicated that she had received only a few victim statements – a very bad sign if we hoped to significantly impact Judge Laura Swain's sentencing decision. Indeed, the situation was actually much worse. The court had received DOZENS of statements recommending leniency for Peter.

A portion of the letter is shown on the next page.

Letter received from U.S. Attorney

December 06, 2012

RE: United States v. Defendant(s) Peter Madoff
Case Number 2009R02082 and Court Docket Number 10-CR-00228

The enclosed information is provided by the United States Department of Justice Victim Notification System (VNS). As a victim witness professional with the United States Attorney's Office, my role is to assist you with information and services during the prosecution of this case. I am contacting you because you were identified by law enforcement as a victim during the investigation of the above criminal case. It is helpful for the Court to know the impact of this crime on its victims. In an effort to provide this information to the Court, we are enclosing a Victim Impact Statement. If you choose to complete a statement, please forward it to:

> Wendy Olsen
> United States Attorneys Office
> USAO - Southern District of New York
> One St. Andrews Plaza
> New York, NY 10007

This is one way the Court can hear your concerns as they relate to the crime. A United States Probation Officer may also contact you in an effort to obtain additional victim impact information. Victim impact information is generally not public information; however, under criminal law and procedures, all information contained in your questionnaire will be disclosed to the defendant and his attorney.

The sentencing hearing for defendant(s), Peter Madoff, has been set for December 20, 2012, 04:30 PM at Clerk's Office, 500 Pearl Street, New York, NY 10007 before Judge Laura Swain. You are welcome to attend this proceeding; however, unless you have received a subpoena, your attendance is not required by the Court. If you plan on attending, you may want to verify the date and time by using the VNS Call Center or web site. If you are a victim of the charged offense(s) and wish to speak at sentencing, please call our office well in advance of the scheduled hearing date.

The sentencing will take place in courtroom 26A.

A United States Probation Officer prepares a report for the Court and may contact you to discuss the impact the crime had on you financially, physically, and/or emotionally. If you are contacted, please make every effort to provide accurate and detailed information.

My mother and I mounted an email effort to gain support for a letter writing campaign to the judge. This resulted in 41 letters by the time of the hearing. There were 63 letters supporting Peter.

In addition to writing an impact statement I asked to speak at the hearing. The press reported that Peter Madoff's attorneys arranged a plea deal with the justice department. Peter would serve no more than 10 years in prison and agreed to forfeit all assets. The plea also included a fine in the symbolic amount of $143.1 billion. This represented all of the money that justice estimated ran through the IA business. Peter Madoff and his family would lose the Westbury, Conn. mansion, the Park Avenue condo, the 1995 Ferrari Spyder and 1958 Aston Martin plus many other tangible assets. He and the family would also forfeit $10 million in cash.

Peter Madoff is only 67; a ten year sentence means that he will likely once again be a free man. A call to Wendy Olsen indicated that the judge did have some leeway in sentencing. I hoped a good turnout and a compelling victim statement during the hearing might influence the judge to increase the sentence to ensure that Peter would never again escape from the penal system.

Unlike the Bernard hearing that was attended by scores of victims and approximately 300 members of the press; the Peter Madoff hearing was more sedate, and less well attended. You will understand the reason for the relatively poor victim turnout in the next chapter. Approximately 20 victims attended; only two spoke at the hearing. I counted 31 members of the press. Peter Madoff attended with his attorneys – there were no family members and no supporters at the hearing.

My victim impact statement to the judge was to be my statement during the hearing. I read it aloud several times and found that it timed out at 9 minutes.

Judge Swain's opening comments indicated that the two speaking to the court should limit their statement to THREE MINUTES. **Panic time!** Over the next few minutes I edited my remarks, dropping entire paragraphs in an attempt to get down to something under five minutes and still maintain the coherence of the statement. My entire victim impact statement is shown below.

December 20, 2012

Wendy Olsen
United States Attorneys Office
USAO - Southern District of New York
One St. Andrews Plaza
New York, NY 10007

RE: United States v. Defendant(s) Peter Madoff
Case Number 2009R02082 and Court Docket Number 10-CR-00228

Victim statement for sentencing hearing of Peter Madoff

Dear Judge Laura Swain:

Your honor, I cannot thank you enough to again have the opportunity to be in a courtroom where a person with the surname Madoff is to be sentenced. Making crime victims part of the process affords those like myself a voice in the criminal justice system. I appeal to this court to access punishment commensurate with the damage this crime caused the victims.

Financial crimes are <u>violent</u> crimes to the victims. Those involved must be punished with significant jail time and not token fines that are a tiny fraction of the amount stolen and often considered nothing more than a cost of doing business. If you *want to change behavior - put the thieves in jail for a long time. The prospect that incarceration is certain will truly deter future crimes like this.*

While the scope of the Madoff Investment Advisory business was global in nature, the emotional and financial damage was done to tens of thousands of innocent <u>individuals, just like me</u>.   I followed the rules.   I did the right thing by planning and saving for my future and that of my family by trusting a firm that was regulated and examined by a Federal agency.

By continuing this crime for decades, Bernard Madoff and his co-conspirators ensured that the innocents would suffer maximum long-term damage with insufficient remaining time to save and recover from the massive theft.

While responsibility for failure to discover this crime can be laid at the feet of those who failed in their obligation to regulate and police SEC regulated brokerages, it is quite clear that the responsibility for designing and running the day-to-day operation of the scandal are Bernard Madoff's inner circle of co-conspirators.

Four years ago Bernard Madoff told us he committed the largest financial crime in the history of the nation by defrauding tens of thousands of innocent victims.   Bernard told us that he did it all by himself. He said that no one else knew, and no one else helped.

It is beyond belief that Madoff <u>alone</u> carried out a crime lasting decades, involving hundreds of feeder fund money raisers, tens of thousands of investors and printing hundreds of thousands of stock confirmations and monthly statements. I believe it to be physically impossible for a single person to carry out such a gargantuan task – all by himself. Bernard Madoff lied – you can be sure others did too.

We, the innocent victims, have been waiting four years for others to acknowledge their role and accept their responsibility for this massive crime. We are still waiting!

Today, the SIPC trustee tells us that Bernard Madoff lied when he says he acted alone. Bernard's claim that he did it "all by himself" is nothing more than an attempt to protect his family from prosecution by giving them an opportunity to claim "plausible deniability." Contrary to Bernard's statement, litigation filed by the trustee suggests that Bernard did indeed have a lot of help.

Irving Picard submits that the 17th floor of the Lipstick building was a den of thieves working together on a daily basis to steal the financial security of those who entrusted this team with their hard earned savings and financial future.

Peter Madoff was one of those persons working on the 17th floor. Not only did he work there — he ran the place. He was trained as an attorney and started to work at the firm in 1965. Peter held the title of "Senior Managing Director and Chief Compliance Officer." Not only was he the owner's brother, but he had been with the firm for decades and held a title indicating he had significant responsibility and oversight for running the business and interacting with the SEC. Yet, Peter tells us that he did not know anything about the criminal enterprise his brother was running; even though the Ponzi scheme operated for decades on the floor where Peter was the "Senior Managing Director." Just what was he directing! There WAS NO LEGITIMATE BUSINESS on that floor — only a vast criminal enterprise printing paper and cashing checks.

Unlike many of his victims, Peter did benefit greatly from the Ponzi scheme. The trustee tells us Peter made a lot of money from his investment account with Bernard. Peter deposited just $32,146 into his account — and he took out $16,252,004. It is breathtaking and incredulous that one could grow thirty-two THOUSAND into sixteen MILLION; an impossibility if the money were truly invested in the market. To someone with Peter's investment experience – it should have set off flashing lights and alarm bells. But it didn't – likely because he knew exactly what was going on.

Peter could have come forward and stopped this crime much earlier thereby greatly limiting the financial damage done to "his customers." He chose not to! The entire investment advisory team waited and waited – until the scheme collapsed. Then they played the part of three blind mice – hear no evil, see no evil and do no evil.

I personally know many Madoff investors and am all too familiar with the impact of this crime on their lives as well as my own. The devastation includes changes not only to how innocent people live, but also to how they die. The press tells us of those who committed suicide because they could not live with the ramifications of this crime. But few talk about the slow death many now experience as the joy in their lives evaporates and they deal with the daily turmoil of destitution caused directly by the crew running and prospering by Bernard Madoff's criminal enterprise.

We will never know how many lives have been shortened by this crime. We can be sure that medical complications as well as emotional trauma and financial considerations have led many to change their day to day lives in a way that reduced both their quality and length of life.

All of this was preventable – if only ONE person was willing to do the right thing and stop this in its tracks years ago. Peter Madoff could have been that person. But he wasn't! In reality, he **chose** not to be the one to end this crime spree.

Peter did eventually plead guilty to something – but not to knowing anything about the Ponzi scheme. Prosecutors allowed a plea agreement where Peter admitted to conspiracy, falsifying records, filing false tax returns and lying to investigators. He never acknowledged he knew what Bernard was doing!

I ask that you show the same degree of compassion to Peter Madoff that he showed to us – <u>none!</u> I and my 84 year other mother are not the only ones impacted. These funds were to be multigenerational in nature targeted toward expenditures such as education, homes and medical expenses.

Many victims are elderly. Many are retired. I planned to retire in January of 2010; now I will <u>never</u> retire. Consider the difficulties of returning to work and finding a job when you are in your 60's, 70's, or even 80's. Consider the impact of a retirement supported only by social security payments.

You have the opportunity to give us justice when you sentence Peter Madoff.

At the same time, you have an opportunity to send Wall Street a message that the white collar crime of defrauding investors will result in much more than a fine or slap on the wrist. Just like Bernard received the maximum, if somewhat symbolic, sentence of 150 years, I ask that you set aside whatever plea arrangement Peter made and impose the maximum sentence possible. Judge Swain, you must serve as the voice of victims when you sentence Peter Madoff. Consider that Peter's investors are serving a life sentence – with no plea deal.

*For the past 4 years, we, the victims still have not heard one person say <u>**"I knew and I am sorry."**</u>*

We deserve better.

Judge Swain made a lengthy statement prior to sentencing. It was at this time that I discovered the option to modify the sentence was actually limited to REDUCING prison time – not INCREASING it.

Peter pleaded guilty to two counts, each with a maximum sentence of five years. I assume that is how the plea agreement yielded 10 years maximum - provided the judge did not use a lower number and if the terms were served consecutively.

I held my breath – it was possible for Peter Madoff to get MUCH LESS than 10 years. If the judge used the maximum and indicated the terms should be served concurrently - Peter would get only FIVE YEARS. It could be even worse if the term was less than the maximum and also concurrent.

A minor victory: Judge Swain gave Peter Madoff the full ten years. I consider that a small victory and worth the effort to travel to New York and speak at the trial. I am not at all certain that the victim impact letters or the two "speakers" made ANY difference at all. The entire hearing may have been little more than a showcase event with the result already decided.

A major defeat: Judge Swain had one last opportunity to punish Peter Madoff. His attorneys asked the judge to postpone incarceration until after his granddaughter's bat mitzvah in early 2013. This was a major gift for what victims consider one of the major henchmen in this crime. Our preference would be to have him handcuffed at the trial and taken away for the next 10 years. The judge ordered Peter Madoff to report on February 6th. There was an audible gasp in the courtroom from the victims. Peter never showed such consideration to them.

THE major victory: Judge Swain gave a lengthy discussion of the case prior to issuing the final sentence. Peter Madoff claimed he did not know it was a Ponzi scheme until after December 11th. Apparently the justice department felt it could not prove a higher level of awareness and complicity "beyond a reasonable doubt" and agreed to this sweetheart plea arrangement. Judge

Swain made several statements in her remarks which I feverishly wrote down. The judge said she <u>did not believe</u> Peter knew nothing about the fraud, calling his lack of admission "frankly not believable." The judge further encouraged Peter Madoff "to tell the truth" during his time in prison.   The judge read from notes saying "Peter Madoff's role was not at all passive" and "Peter Madoff did nothing in the way of oversight. But still worse than doing nothing to oversee the operation, he lied to authorities." The judge telling the world that she did not believe Peter was unexpected and greatly appreciated.   It also makes the leniency shown by allowing him to remain a free man to attend a family event all the more inexplicable.

Peter Madoff was also permitted to make a statement.

> "I am deeply ashamed of my conduct, I accept full responsibility for my actions."

Notice that he never addressed the victims in attendance, and he never said "I am sorry for what I did to you."

Like Ruth Madoff who kept $2.5 million, Peter Madoff and his family agreed to forfeit all of their assets. Peter's wife, Marion, was allowed to keep $771,000 in cash.   For a Madoff this must have seemed like pocket change.

It is important to mention the second speaker.   Unlike my case where the name "Madoff" was nothing more than the characters written in ink and printed on the statements I received over the years, this woman actually knew **all** of the Madoffs personally. The families had attended birthday parties, weddings and other social functions. For her, the betrayal was very personal.

Below are a few additional comments from various victim statements.   These comments show the breath of damage not just to the current generation, but also to future generations of a family.

"Four years ago on December 11, 2008 we were comfortably retired in Maine. The phone rang and it was my husband's daughter saying that we had lost all of our money due to a ponzi scheme engineered by Bernard Madoff, which our whole family was invested in, brothers, sisters, grandmothers, grandfathers, aunts and uncles, all lost everything.

Our now life is discount stores and living as inexpensively as we can. Will we be able to support ourselves in our "golden years" -- we cannot plea bargain that reality away.

I am now 90 years old and bankrupt. I have been waiting hopelessly to recover the money Madoff stole from me. At the very least, I expected to receive some compensation from my SIPC insurance. Four years have passed and I have received nothing and, I see no help coming from the U.S. Department of Justice.

Peter and Bernard Madoff didn't just take my money, they took my sense of security, they took my freedom, my independence and they took my peace of mind,

I feel as if I've written this letter in various forms over the last four years, and I'm not sure why I bother. However, here we go again."

I plan to contact the U.S. Attorney and ask to be kept informed of all future plea discussions so that we, the victims, have time to impact the discussions and suggest a more severe punishment than the sweet deal given to Peter Madoff.

After the hearing, Peter Madoff exited the courthouse, walked pass the cameras and reporters, got into a gray BMW - and drove away.

The second Madoff was going to jail – eventually!

The bottomless pit and the gift that keeps giving!

Following is a summary of what we have covered thus far.

The trustee alleges many others were involved in the scheme. Including details recounting the excesses and 'grab for the gold ring' by individuals including Frank DiPascali, Daniel Bonventre, Charles Weiner and Joane Crupi appear overkill. Including more about specific individuals would not add to this story of greed, avarice and distain for the rule of law and utter disregard for the welfare of IA customers.

Let's take a quick review of the bounty showered on insiders who benefited so much from this crime.

1. Salaries, bonuses and commissions well in excess of industry standards.
2. Gratuitous loans, which never required repayment, for homes, hunting memberships, boats, credit cards etc.
3. The "magic" accounts which were never funded with any money – yet returned millions in "profits".
4. The "time machine" accounts reporting gains as much as 18 months BEFORE the account was opened.
5. Returns for preferred non-split-strike accounts generated profits that were not only out of this world, but out of this universe.

Only in the imaginary world of Bernard Madoff would seasoned professionals believe any of this was real. The imagery of deaf, dumb and blind is totally inadequate to explain the degree of negligence, lack of oversight and willingness to flout regulations repeatedly exhibited by IA employees and other co-conspirators.

This book presented you with very detailed information about the formation and execution of the Madoff crime. You can draw your own conclusion about what insiders knew and their degree of complicity in Madoff's scheme. I have drawn mine.

My own personal opinion is - <u>they all knew</u> .

Criminal law requires "beyond a reasonable doubt" rather than "a preponderance of the evidence" – I assume the U.S. Attorney's office simply cannot prove guilt in a court of law.

Madoff was never discovered by regulatory authorities. The great liquidity crisis of 2008 leading to an accompanying inability to raise (perhaps steal is a better word) sufficient amounts of new money to meet investor redemptions finally ended the scam.

By this point your head is in all probability spinning with the level of detail and heavy reliance on numbers to make points and draw conclusions. Just remember, this book was written by someone who makes a living by collecting, interpreting and reporting numbers. Take some comfort in the fact that you have been subjected to less than half of the material used in the class.

Now it is time to leave the fantasy world of Madoff's fictional IA business and enter the nightmare world he created for his investors.

It is time to focus on the more important players in this story – the true victims – you, me and anyone who thinks they can trust the U.S. Securities industry.

For the remainder of this book and throughout Volume II of this series I will be your personal escort on a journey through the intricate maze created by regulatory authorities and agencies tasked with addressing the great injustices inflicted on victims of this horrendous crime. If you were never involved in a crime like this you cannot truly comprehend the difficulties faced by victims trying to understand what happened, why it happened, why it wasn't discovered and the barriers victims face trying to recover from this disaster. Rather than improving the situation, regulatory agencies continually place roadblocks in the path of victims. In many cases investors are made to feel more like criminals than crime victims.

After nearly four years of facing insurmountable obstacles I have few illusions as to the inexorable final outcome.

9 DEMORALIZED, DISPIRITED AND RESIGNED

One door closes as the Madoff financial crime ceases operations in December of 2008.   Another door immediately opens as victims learn damages will be measured in more than just monetary losses.

Confidence in the system we have been told by our government to use to build wealth vanished as Madoff investors realized that those who make the rules in this game planned to deny most investors any monetary compensation.   Legislators who tell us they are there to represent and protect the middle class from Wall Street excesses are routinely inaccessible and regularly fail to support legislation that would help us now and also protect future investors.

Several books have been published about the Madoff Ponzi scheme. Books written by detached journalists and academics whose authors have long since moved on to the next story simply cannot match the daily immersion and consuming passion of someone living with the repercussions of this crime for almost four years.

Madoff investors, as well as those involved in other large financial crimes, are going to have a very difficult time achieving any significant monetary recovery. Opportunities for recovery are few while roadblocks are many. Wall Street, and unfortunately the political and regulatory system, is stacked against the individual investor. The "system" has an endless supply of money, time and access to the news media and Congress.

Time is an issue; many will not live long enough to see the trustee complete the distribution of recovered assets. Money is an issue; lawyers are expensive and few see any benefit in pro-bono work for victims that are often despised by so many Americans. Access to members of Congress is an issue; access by financially ravaged investors is extremely limited - Wall Street has the money and power to impose its will. During election cycles politicians of both parties often march hand-in-hand with "the average American" promising to represent the interests of the middle class. This behavior is meant to do one thing – secure your vote. With few exceptions, that "pat on the back" during an election cycle is the only contact you will have with Congress! Energy is an issue; Madoff victims, many already elderly, are getting older both chronologically and emotionally as they face the very real prospect of little or no progress in advancing their agenda.

This book, written by one so intimately involved, affords you the opportunity to become a part of the underworld of the "Madoff experience." Through my experiences, you will begin to understand the nature of those investing with Madoff and the series of tumultuous events that turned their lives upside down. I want you to grasp the significance of this event which caused so much damage to the lives of tens of thousands victimized first by Madoff and then by the system ostensibly put in place to protect them (obviously this failed) and compensate them (this function too has failed most victims).   The Madoff event is significant not just to his victims, but to every current and future Wall Street investor.

A life altering event

Only one-quarter of Madoff's investors were institutional organizations such as pensions and charities.   Three quarters were individuals making this a personal tragedy very close to home for many families.

For those who have not yet retired (like me) - imagine decades of planning for a sound financial retirement instantaneously proving itself to be worthless!   All those deposits into an investment account and all those statements reporting increased retirement assets simply evaporating into thin air in a heartbeat.   There is not enough time left to start over.   There is no opportunity to work long enough or save enough to create a nest egg adequate to supplement social security benefits.   A comfortable retirement has become an unreachable fantasy. Retiring at all, at any time, is no longer possible.

Suppose that you (or a parent or grandparent) were already retired and receiving both social security and a pension check. Further assume the pension check represents 75% of total income.   One day, without any advance warning, the pension component just stops.   How would your life change if you lost three quarters of your income?   You may consider going back to work but finding a job when you have been out of the workforce for years will be challenging if not downright impossible for a 60, or 70, or even 80 year old.

It is not just the current account holder that suffers.   Many families had multigenerational Madoff accounts.   Assets managed by Madoff were often passed from grandparent, to parent, to child, to grandchild (of course the account would be diminished by payment of the Federal estate and State inheritance taxes over time). These assets often constituted the bulk of wealth passed to descendants and would be targeted for housing, medical, education or other family expenses. Everything stopped on the day Madoff's scheme collapsed. Those families must now find another source of funding for these expenses – or maybe they won't!

There is a reason for the current state of despair by Madoff investors/victims. These investors clearly have not made their case with the American public at large. It has been four years since the arrest of Bernard Madoff. The effort to inform and educate the public about the specifics of the case and the nature of the victims has proven largely unsuccessful as evidenced by the comments below.

The sentencing hearing for Peter Madoff on December 20th, 2012 led to a flurry of news reports. Many of those news reports received comments to the online articles. Clearly, the "blame the victim" mentality persists. Is it any wonder that many victims now refuse to talk to the press? This book is one additional, and perhaps last, attempt to gain not your sympathy, but your understanding.

> *"At first I felt sorry for the people who invested with this fraud, but now I feel that investors themselves seeking to make a lot of money for which they didn't really earn are also somewhat committing fraud themselves.*
>
> *If it sounds too good to be true, it probably is a Ponzi scheme! If you have the kind of money it takes to invest in a Madoff scam, you need to be smart enough to ask questions!*
>
> *It's all about greed. The victims happily gave their money to Madoff for a return on their money much higher than*

elsewhere putting caution to the wind on illusions of fantastic wealth."

Of course, not all comments were negative. Some do "get it."

"More naiive than greedy. Actually Madoff promised a consistent return of 10% a year, when some mutual funds were returning 20% plus in some of those same years during the 80s and 90s. Hedge funds scoff at 10%. You can't blame the victims. Bernie successfully portrayed himself as a highly skilled but conservative money manager. A lot of very smart people gave him their money."

10 THE STEREOTYPE OF THE MADOFF INVESTOR

The news media did victims a great disservice by airing clips from those incessantly describing "wealthy Madoff investors who got what they deserved." The stereotype is wrong! Madoff had tens of thousands of investors. Although only a few thousand had direct brokerage accounts, many thousands more were invested through feeder funds. It has proven very difficult to overcome the negative image created in those first few weeks after Madoff's arrest. Rather than evoking sympathy in other Americans, Madoff victims have too often experienced scorn and contempt.

In an attempt to correct these widespread misperceptions twenty-nine investors collaborated on a book titled "The Club No One Wanted to Join." It took a great deal of courage to participate in this endeavor since it entailed exposing your identify to the public. This book describes, in often graphic details, the before and after lives of these investors. My mother and I were contributors to this book. Our stories, like all 27 others in this book, describe "the real Madoff investor"; which is starkly different than the media evoked stereotype. I am including the two stories of my family in this new book because I believe it gives you a real insight into the personal lives of two investors. These stories also prepare you for the material in this book which gives you an insight into how victims coped with the news and how the Madoff scandal ruined lives and stole futures. You should understand that my story, and that of my mother, is NOT unique. Should you read "The Club No One Wanted to Join" (which I highly recommend) you will find 27 other stories of average Americans – just like you!

Although the book includes stories about 29 "of the willing", the chapters in this book could have been written by any of Madoff's victims. If you ever have the misfortune to find yourself in a similar predicament – you could easily join the ranks and write your story. I sincerely hope that you receive a warmer and more compassionate welcome from your fellow citizens than Madoff victims encountered.

"Rags To Riches, To Rags, (Emma)

I am a product of the Great Depression. I learned to never buy anything you cannot pay for, never live beyond your means, and always save for the future.

Shortly after I was born in 1928, my parents packed up the family and moved to Florida. This was to be a new beginning for the family and the start of a new business that would allow my father to support a growing family. There would eventually be ten children. Today, only the two survive; I the oldest, and my sister, the youngest.

My father made arrangements to run two different businesses in Florida. One was to run an apartment complex named the "Cadillac Apartments." This business was to provide a regular, predictable income for the family. The real prize was to purchase a mahogany Chris Craft speed boat and run it as a tourist attraction. Initially things went well with both businesses and eventually the revenue from the speed boat became the primary source of income for the family.

This ended abruptly when the boat broke down several miles offshore and was towed in by the Coast Guard. There were large swells that day and the boat was broached by a wave and eventually sank. There was no insurance and insufficient money to purchase another boat. Other family issues back home became pressing at about the same time and we again packed up the family; this time moving north back to Philadelphia. At this point the family consisted of two children.

We moved to an apartment in Philadelphia and my father got a job working for a contractor that painted homes. This is when the family really started to grow. A new child was born every two years. As the family grew we moved several time to larger quarters – always as renters. With the larger family came more pressure on income. The oldest kids took local jobs cleaning horse stalls, collecting roadside metals that could be sold to a junk yard and selling flowers that we grew ourselves and pastries that my mother made in her kitchen.

My father wanted one more opportunity to start his own business. Taking our savings we once again packed up the family and move to Franklinville, New Jersey, where my father leased a farm and purchased several thousand chickens. We needed six months to allow the chickens to grow to a sufficient size to sell. We almost made it. Just a few weeks before our "sell date", the chicken coup became infested with a disease that killed half the chickens. We lost the farm and moved back to Philadelphia. There were now six children.

World War II came along and my father got a job working at the Frankford Arsenal in Philadelphia making munitions for the war effort. The eighth child came along. This new child was born with mental issues, became very sick and nearly died. While he did recover, he was never able to function as a normal adult. His treatment by the school system, government and society in general was much different than what someone with his disability would face today.

My father changed jobs again as the war approached the midway point. He worked in the paint shop at the Philadelphia Navy Yard and received a significant increase in salary. This increase was absolutely necessary as the family continued to grow.

I was now 14 and permitted to leave school to help with family finances. In those days, children went to work and brought their money home to the father of the household – all of it. I was given a small allowance, but the real objective of my quitting school and working was to support the younger children in the household.

WWII was fast approaching a successful conclusion. Things were looking bright for the family. Then my father started to have stomach problems. Over the next few years we had a series of trips to doctors. But my father never really seemed to get better.

He passed away in 1947 from cancer that was never clearly diagnosed or treated.

The tenth child was born weeks before my father passed away.   I was 19.

The burden for supporting ten kids fell upon my mother, the widow, and the oldest children.

The objective became to make the most money you could regardless of whether you liked the job or not. I started to work at a factory. My oldest brother went to work at Bond Bread and my mother worked on assembling TV sets.

It was at Bond Bread that my brother met several returning veterans who recently started working at the company. One of these vets eventually became my husband of 60 years. It truly was love at first sight. Most men would have run the other way when he saw a family with 10 kids and a widow. My husband did not. He was an instant hit with the older kids and a sensation with the younger ones. He talked of getting married in two months and asked me if it would be OK to have a large family. He came from a family of eight. After the experience of being "the mom" for my younger brothers and sisters at the age of only 14, I told him that "if you want a large family, then you need a different girl." Again, he did not run away.

We married in 1949 and bought a small house near my mom. My first child was born fifteen months after we got married. Just as in the past, my younger brothers and sisters became our extended family. Our own children, plus this extended family became the "large" family that my husband always wanted.

My husband's family was "wealthy." They had a small 600 sq ft home in Wildwood Villas and we spent many happy years in that home playing cards, catching and cooking crabs with spaghetti and growing a little vegetable garden.

Things were going extremely well.   My mother's kids were now all grown up and I was beginning my own family.   The job at Bond Bread seemed secure (after all, people would always eat bread) and my husband was now a shop foreman.

There was still a draft in place and all of the men on both sides of the family were either drafted or joined the military.   My husband's father was one of the "doughboys" who volunteered to fight for the allies in World War I.   He eventually would serve in the trenches outside of Paris and received the Purple Heart for wounds received during one offensive.

Then along came the Cold War, Korea and Vietnam.   Members of my family served in every U.S. conflict from WWI right through the Gulf War.   You will recognize the names of some of the places and battles where they fought including Guam, Saipan, Bastogne, Inchon, Khe-Sahn, Fallujah, and the Atlantic convoys transporting war materials from the U.S. to Britian.   Our men served as riflemen, MPs, sailors, electricians, airmen and paratroopers.   None were officers; all were regular Americans who did their duty when called to serve.   With the exception of my sixty year old son who served as a Naval airman, all of our personal "heroes" are now gone. My son was also a Madoff victim.

My mother passed away in 1982.

By this time I moved from Philadelphia to the suburbs. My daughter moved there just a few months earlier and I, like my mother, wanted to be near my children and grandchildren.

Life was grand. After 22 years working for Sears, I quit and went to work in my son's business.

In the early 1990's my son discussed a new investment opportunity and we both opened an account with a firm named Avellino and Bienes. In 1992 this was converted to an account with Bernard Madoff Investment Securities following an SEC investigation that led to the closure of the Avellino and Bienes firm and the implied recommendation that Madoff was a very well respected money manager and that his firm was one of the largest in the NASDAQ.

Beginning in 1998 my husband and I started to travel. I had never flown before and had a great fear of getting into an airplane. My daughter and son-in-law scheduled a family to Florida and we went along. I took a nerve pill and got on the airplane – one shaky step at a time. It was absolutely an exhilarating experience. Flying opened up a whole new world. In the next four years we traveled to

Alaska, California and the Caribbean.

We were getting older now – and no one lives forever. Our goal was that this investment account would be used to replace the income from social security and pension for the one who passed first. I thought that would be me. My husband was absolutely NEVER sick.

It is now 2002 and our future and retirement looks very secure. My husband retired from his job as the building superintendent at the YMCA, and my grandchildren were in the process of starting their own families. We decided to set 2005 as our final retirement year and begin to live on our investment with Madoff.

But as always, fate plays a part in every life. Even the best laid plans, no matter how well thought out, are subject to human fragilities. In early 2004 my husband got quite ill. This was eventually diagnosed as multiple myeloma – which is incurable. The next years were a whirlwind of doctors, tests and treatment. The medication of choice to treat his cancer was thalidomide (yes the old drug from the 50's that was initially used for pregnant women). It was VERY expensive, costing more than $5,000 per month. This was a complex disease. I kept a loose leaf folder where I recorded notes for every doctor seen, every test taken, every medication prescribed, every hospital visit and every operation. The book eventually grew to over 300 pages and I firmly believe that the *information in this book that tied all of these various entities together extended my husband's life and reinforced my understanding of the disease. In 2007 we made our one and only withdrawal from the Madoff account – to pay for medical bills. Eventually, in 2008 my husband succumbed to the disease and he passed away.*

The time had come to implement "the plan." Over the course of the next seven months my family and I completed the necessary paperwork to finalize my husband's estate. On December 8th I was in the office of my local bank arranging to close the Madoff account and begin living on the income from a two decade investment. It was not meant to be.

Although my son found out about the Madoff arrest late in the evening of December 11, 2008, he did not tell me about it for three more days. I believe he was trying to spare me the pain of knowing that my life would never be the same and that the goals and plans discussed years ago would never come to pass.

I simply could not believe that all those brokerage account statements, stock transaction statements and 1099s reporting all my "earnings" were nothing more than tissue paper.

Madoff, the monster, had stolen my life.

Now, rather than "living the plan", I live with a

dramatically different lifestyle with very different objectives and with a very different "job."

My new "job" is communicating with others who were victimized by Madoff to attempt to recover some small portion of my investment. A significant part of my remaining income, which is largely Social Security, is devoted to accountants and attorneys who advise me about things that need to be done to address the Madoff fraud. I cannot spend my entire limited income on myself – I continue to spend way too much on Madoff.

I spend hours each week on the phone with legislators in an attempt to recover the major source of monies available to me – taxes paid for two decades on fraudulent 1099 income. I simply cannot understand how the government can keep this money. Only a morally bankrupt society would keep taxes collected as a result of a criminal activity.

I spend hours reading the news items that describe in sickening detail the role that the SEC played in allowing Madoff to perpetrate this fraud for so long.

And, I hope and pray, that our elected legislators "come through" for us and do the right and moral thing. Our government played a huge role in perpetuating the Madoff fraud and they need to do all they can to make it right.

*My life has changed in a number of ways, none
of which could have been imagined in 1990,
1992 or even 2008 when my husband passed.*

> *I wanted to put central air in my home
> to make it more appealing when I sell
> it.*

> *I wanted to buy a hybrid car to replace
> the one that my husband routinely
> drove.*

> *I shop with coupons and check all the
> ads before I buy something.*

> *It is cheaper to go the second hand
> store to buy clothes.*

> *I turn the thermostat down and sit near
> an electric heater so I do not have to
> heat the entire house*

> *I am 81 – my years are coming to an
> end. I will have little if anything left in
> my estate to pass along to my heirs*

*In some ways I am one of the fortunate Madoff
investors. I still have my very supportive family.
Thank God for the Madoff group. It has been
not just a source of information but also a
source of inspiration. Like most in the group, I
find myself supporting the objectives of others
just because it is the right thing to do, not
because it will benefit me personally.*

I may have lost my money, but I am still rich.

I want my fellow Americans to gain a better understanding of what the real Madoff investor looks like. You need to understand that we did nothing wrong other than listening to the agency that is tasked by congress with protecting me against this type of fraud. So far, my country, thru the SEC, has failed me. I hope that your country will not fail you.

My story is that of the typical American family —just like the story you would be telling me about your family.

I have a message for you – and I hope you are willing to listen."

My mother is an amazing woman. As you have read, her approach to life was conditioned by her family experience during the Great Depression. She worked very hard to succeed in a world very different and very less family focused than the one she grew up in. Like every other American, her goal was to prepare her children for a life better than her own.

"Starting with the American Dream, Ending with the Nightmare of Retirement", (Michael)

Growing up in Philadelphia my family first lived in a 3 bedroom row home of about 900 square feet. My sister and I went to a local Catholic grade school, my father worked on the assembly line at a local electronics company, and my mom was a stay at home mother until we were old enough for school. Once we were in school my mom worked in customer service at Sears for more than two decades.

Summers were spent taking weekend trips to my grandparents' home at the Jersey Shore. Fishing, half ball, biking and roller skating with neighborhood kids constituted entertainment.

At a very early age, I was instilled with the value of earning your own money and learned the security of living within your means while saving for a comfortable retirement. Starting at about the age of eight I earned money by delivering local sales circulars along with other kids in the neighborhood. When I reached 10 years old my father and I wallpapered homes in the area to earn extra money. Summer jobs included working at Sears and other local department stores in the shipping department. My first savings account was at the church Credit Union. My parents insisted that half of the amount I earned at any job had to be deposited into this savings account. This began a lifetime habit of saving for the future.

After completing school and serving six years in the Navy I worked at a research firm that specialized in sophisticated statistical analysis and forecasting. Many new statistical techniques were developed and 60 hour work weeks were commonplace. I did not earn a lot, but I did learn a lot.

In 1982 I formed my own research company. This new company required the purchase of a very expensive computer and represents the *one and only time in my life that I took out a loan for something other than a mortgage or health care. I borrowed $75,000 for the computer to run the new business. The purchase of this computer precluded incurring further debt for an office. Therefore the very large computer was located in the dining room of my home. This was truly a "home office." A few years later, "my staff" was comprised of myself and both of my parents. The company was very successful and within just a few years the computer was totally paid for.*

It became clear that this company could generate quite a bit of revenue. If we worked very hard, continued to live our very conservative life style, and saved everything else we would be able to set aside sufficient funds for a comfortable, financially secure future. At the age of 35 I could see that bank account balances were growing very rapidly.

Over the next few years I began to diversify away from bank accounts and CDs and moved into a brokerage account. I found the results of this foray were not particularly successful, predictable or profitable. Returns varied widely from double digit annual gains to double digit losses. I was looking for something with a reasonable and predictable rate of return. I was absolutely willing to accept limited upside gains in order to avoid a large downside risk.

In 1990 a colleague at the university computer center introduced me to a firm named Avellino *and Bienes. A&B invested in some type of interest bearing investment with a return of about 10%. About 18 months after I opened an account the SEC investigated A&B. The news media reported that the SEC suspected A&B was running a Ponzi scheme. The SEC investigation indicated that the firm was operating as an unlicensed investment advisory which led to the SEC fining A&B and closing the firm. The investment, plus interest, in A&B was returned to me and other investors. A Wall Street Journal article in late 1992 indicated that the real brains behind the A&B investments were from a firm named Bernard Madoff Investment Securities in N.Y. A&B was actually just collecting money from a number of sources, giving it to Madoff and taking a percentage. The article indicated that the total size of the A&B investments were about $400 million. The money invested with A&B was moved to Madoff's brokerage firm. My parents and I each opened an account, funding it initially with the money returned from A&B.*

The Madoff investment seemed much more secure than A&B. I now knew that the SEC had blessed Madoff Investment Securities in the WSJ. I learned that the investment advisor, Bernard Madoff was a former chairman of the NASDAQ and that his brokerage firm did a very large trading volume, as much as 15% of the total daily volume on the NASDAQ exchange.

I also felt a much greater level of comfort with this investment. Unlike A&B that simply listed an interest payment on "something", I now had a brokerage statement each month that showed purchases and sales of Fortune 500 company stock along with S&P 100 option contracts.

At this point I was 42 and my company was doing very well and generating substantial profits. My parents and I developed a plan with two objectives.

For my parents the plan was for the BLMIS investment to grow to a point where it would replace the lost income from pension and social security payments once one of them passed. For me, the goal was for the investment to grow to a point where I could retire earlier than 65 with sufficient income to maintain my existing lifestyle.

For the next decade we watched the investment grow at a predictable rate averaging about 10.5% per year. We continued to live below our means and add to the investment of a regular investment – never making a withdrawal. A statistical forecasting analysis indicated that full retirement for my parents would occur in 2005 and I could retire in February of 2010. The last investment of new capital was made in 2002.

This decade of 1992 to 2002 became one of the best in my life. I spent my time traveling for business and visited some of the most beautiful locations in the world. I learned to play tennis and formed a lasting friendship with a group of men who played tennis most mornings. My mother took her first ever plane flight and my parents eventually traveled to places including Alaska, California, Florida and the Caribbean. The future was bright, and financial independence was all but guaranteed. While the Madoff account never provided the huge positive returns reported in some years by some mutual funds (sometimes reporting annual returns of 30% plus) it also never reported negative returns. I had exactly what I was looking for; I would gladly eschew the very large single year returns in exchange for a reliable and predictable rate of return with limited downside risk.

Something else happened in 2002. Routine medical tests for my father showed some anomalies. Two years later he was in the hospital diagnosed with a relatively rare form of bone marrow cancer.

Beginning in 2004 my family spent significantly more time on medical treatments and the company generated fewer profits. The cancer was incurable. Four years later my father succumbed to the disease, passing in April of 2008. At his funeral, my mother collected the second of her American flags that was placed on the coffin of one who wore the colors of his country. My flag will eventually join those of an uncle who died in Germany and that of my father who served in the Pacific Theatre during WWII.

I spent the next few months talking to accountants, lawyers and other professionals on tax returns and completing my father's estate paperwork.

No one lives forever and the experience of my father indicated that even the best laid plans are subject to human fragilities. He never benefited to any great extent from the 50 years of saving and planning culminating with the BLMIS account.

December 8th of 2008 my mother and I were in the offices of our local bank arranging to close the BLMIS accounts, close down the business and finally retire and use the resources that we accumulated over the past decades years of planning and saving.

Three days later Bernard Madoff was arrested.

For all who invested with Madoff, our lives have never been, and will never be, the same again. This is a nightmare from which I will never awake. All the planning, all the dreams over a period of decades evaporated in the span of a two minute phone call on December 11th at 8:05 p.m. Madoff had been arrested. Madoff told his sons that the whole business was a fraud.

My initial reaction was one of disbelief. I knew that Madoff had two types of clients; those with direct brokerage accounts and those investing through feeder funds (like A&B in 1990). A deep sense of denial caused me to leap to the conclusion that my account was safe because I had these many years of brokerage statements and stock confirmation slips. I assumed that "it was the other guy" with the feeder fund accounts that had been wiped out.

Over the next 24 hours it became clear that the entire investment advisory business was a fraud. The reality slowly dawned that this retirement nest egg was totally gone and absolutely irreplaceable. As I approach 60 years old, my best earning years are behind me. There is no longer sufficient time, energy or even interest in rebuilding assets that would be sufficient in size to allow for a secure retirement.

I did not tell my mother what happened for three days. I simply could not bring myself to tell her that the income from my father's pension and social security were never going to be replaced and that her income was to be reduced by 75% for the remainder of her life.

Over the next month I immersed myself into learning about the sources by which Madoff victims could recover some small portion of their investment.

An article in our local newspaper, the Philadelphia Inquirer, carried a front page article about a Madoff investor currently living in Fl, but a native of my home state of Pa. I eventually searched out that investor and communicated via email and phone over the next few days. Clearly, we were both in the dark about how to proceed. Much more information was needed. Searches on the internet indicated that some Madoff investors were forming a group named "Madoff Survivors" which was meant to serve as a support and information source for Madoff victims. I became one of the early members of this group and began to share information with others. Email activity eventually reached more than 100 per day. No one really knew anything about how to proceed or who, besides Madoff himself, was responsible for this mess.

We did know that we were part of the biggest financial crime in the history of the nation.

I learned very early on that taxes paid on the fraudulent 1099's for two decades were likely to represent the lion's share of any recovery. It became very clear that the only real "winners" were Madoff's cronies and the IRS. Not only did they receive significant revenue from crime victims, but they also benefited in another nefarious way. Madoff and others who likely knew of this crime paid themselves significant salaries. Those salaries were taxed by the IRS. All of the money for salaries and taxes were paid out of the assets of Madoff crime victims.

*The first 90 days were a whirlwind of activity.
Realizing that tax refunds would be an
important source of recovery, I spent significant
time with attorneys and accountants seeking
information for what we could hope to recover.
The early comments were not promising.   It
appeared that federal taxes would be covered
by a theft loss allowing significant "co-pays"
and only going back 3 years.   The investigation
of tax refunds for my state indicated that
recovery options were very limited.   The three
year statue of limitation would continue to run
while the trustee investigated the fraud.   Since
the trustee indicated this could take a decade –
the state of Pa would likely return nothing.*

*By this point the failures of the SEC were
becoming increasingly clear.   While I knew that
the SEC had investigated BLMIS on a number of
occasions I now had more information about
the repeated investigations that were both
incompetent and negligent.   I slowly drew the
conclusion that I was a victim of both Madoff
and my government.   But for the incompetence
and negligence of the SEC, Madoff would have
been discovered in 1992 and his operation shut
down in that year.   It was not A&B that was
running the ponzi scheme; it was Madoff.   And,
the SEC missed the Madoff crime completely in
that 1992 investigation of A&B.   The SEC report
released the first week in September of 2009
cemented the findings that the SEC had indeed
dropped the ball and let us, and every
American, down to such a degree that they*

abetted the largest ponzi scheme in history.

The SEC internal watchdog report painted a picture of an agency that missed many opportunities to discover the fraud. The full 400+ page report painted a picture of an even more nefarious agency where the terms "negligence" and "incompetence" seem far too tame and are woefully inadequate to describe the failures of this agency. On the battlefield, errors of this type by those who lead invariably result in the deaths of those in their command. The failures of the SEC have already resulted in deaths; most famously the suicide of Rene-Thierry Magon de la Villehuchet, of French aristocracy. I am absolutely certain that the SEC failure will lead to premature deaths for many Madoff investors. The current and continuing stresses, both physical and emotional, will continue for the remainder of the lives of all those who were touched by the Madoff crime and the associated failures of the SEC.

This report implicated yet another government agency whose failed investigation of Madoff would result in large losses for Americans—the Internal Revenue Service. In the early 2000's, Madoff applied to the IRS as a non-bank IRA custodian. Surprisingly, and in violation of their own rules, the IRS approved Madoff to handle IRAs. For decades our government encouraged us to invest in our retirement, both with their words and with the tax code. IRAs are sacrosanct in our society, untouchable by almost all creditors. Yet another government failure led to tens of thousands losing their IRA and pension savings due to the Madoff fraud. For most of these investors, our government has yet to do anything to make them whole.

Throughout my life I chose to follow the rules, stay out of trouble, pay my taxes, avoid the press, avoid politics, and focus on friends, family and career. I am one of those faceless Americans that never seek the spotlight and assiduously avoid any event that could provide that elusive "15 minutes of fame." I am nobody; I am everybody; I am the average American. But I now found myself in a new arena where only an activist approach would gain the attention of politicians. In order to succeed I had to do my best to alert other Americans to the plight of Madoff investors, to make them aware of the role of the SEC, and to make them think about the need to address justice and fairness for Madoff investors. Americans need to understand the risks associated with the securities markets that had rained catastrophic ruins on those who did nothing wrong.

I started this newly discovered activism with phone calls, emails and faxes to a variety of sources. I decided early on that the press was to be a primary strategic asset to reach both politicians and the American population.

The stereotype of the average Madoff investor had to be changed from that of the wealthy, Jewish professional who should have known better. It had to be changed to be more reflective of the many thousands of average Americans who invested in our securities markets with a well respected investment manager and were then betrayed by the government agency meant to protect them from exactly this type of fraud.

I began calling politicians in my local area (both federal and state) to ask about the liability of the SEC and our government to address the damages done to American investors by our own government. I also contacted any news agency that would listen and granted every interview requested by the press, both U.S. and foreign.

During the sentencing hearing for Madoff on June 29th, 2008, my mother and I traveled by train to New York. We were accompanied by a reporter and photographer from the Philadelphia Inquirer and met up with a French media team in the subway tunnel in N.Y.

This sentencing hearing was the zenith of interest by the press. It has proven increasingly difficult to gain and maintain the media attention as the press moves on to other issues. I have discovered that the press is an ally that allows us to gain access to those with real power – the political class that writes the laws that controls our fate.

The SEC failed us, and they will fail you. This theme was important, but difficult to convey to the population at large. Only through repeated exposures to the press could we get the message out. All too often these press encounters invariably led to ridicule by those uninformed Americans who saw the news items and blamed the victims because it was easier than trying to understand government involvement in this very complex issue. Most Americans would not even entertain the thought that this could have easily happened to them.

The repeated press encounters, and the thousands of calls, letters and emails to Congress by my mother and I as well as many other members of the Madoff groups has led to some successes.

Congress enacted Revenue Procedure 2009-20 which gives Madoff victims the opportunity to recover Federal taxes paid for up to five years. This is a major improvement over the existing three year limit that was the current regulation. But, is it enough? It still allows our government to benefit financially from a crime since many Madoff investors paid taxes for decades.

I have been working closely with members of the state of Pennsylvania legislature to address the Madoff and other ponzi schemes. We had our own local "mini-Madoff". William Forte (the Pa. Ponzi fraud) victimized almost exclusively local Pennsylvania victims. The state legislator in Forte's district was gracious enough to schedule hearings on the matter in June 2009 and asked if I would be willing to testify in Harrisburg, the state capitol. I was received warmly by the 15 or so legislators in the hearing. On November 17th, 2009, Pennsylvania proposed legislation to return three years of taxes on fraudulent ponzi schemes. This may not seem like much, but under current law I would get nothing.

I have found that working aggressively, being diligent and being persistent does eventually pay off. Sometimes frustration does set in which can lead to an audacious act. For me this meant calling the White House switch board one day and asking to speak directly to the President about Madoff. Not surprisingly, I was not connected. I also wrote to Bernard Madoff in prison. Again this yielded no additional information about how he duped the SEC for decades.

In little ways we try to cut expenses. We painted the entire house ourselves and cut coupons weekly. My mom and I actually enjoyed the experience of painting the interior of the home. It happened early in 2009 as we were approaching the first anniversary of my father's passing. It was a welcome distraction from the loss of someone we desperately missed.

In some ways I wish my father were here to share in this experience that draws us even closer together. In other ways, I am glad that he is not here since the trauma of this great loss would likely have made his disease even more deadly.

Every single victory has been earned. Madoff victims need more. And we need the support of every American that can very easily find themselves in exactly the same situation.

A few weeks ago, a federal judge found that the Army Corps of Engineers was liable to the victims of hurricane Katrina for their negligence in constructing the levees in New Orleans.

I hope that sometime in the near future I will see the following press release: "a federal judge found that the SEC was liable to the victims of the Madoff fraud for their negligence in multiple failed SEC investigations of BLMIS."

I come from a military family. Americans that come from my class wear the colors and fight our wars. For all Americans, mine is the class that sheds your blood and occasionally comes home wearing your flag. I do not come from the class that produces your officers who plan the wars in the Pentagon. I come from the class that provides your trigger pullers. From the doughboy that occupied the trenches in France during WWI to the Marine in Iraq sitting in an armored humvee manning the 50 cal. machine gun, my class serves when called. When the Madoff fraud came to light it was

*time to follow the practice of "fight or flight."
As all American servicemen do when the need
arises, I took up the challenge and made the
decision to fight. Now for the first time in my
life I need my government to answer my call. I
sit here wondering if it will.*

*I never anticipated that this endeavor would
take so much time, effort and energy. I find
myself today much older than would be
expected simply by the passage of a single
year. This has now become a full time job.*

My hopes for the future include the following.

*I hope that Americans come to truly understand
the danger in the markets posed by an
ineffective SEC. I believe that the real story will
eventually come out and that my fellow citizens
will finally come to understand and sympathize
with the Madoff victims and actively engage in
ensuring that they get the justice and fair
treatment by our government that is deserved.
I hope that those who were directly involved or
who knew of this fraud are brought to justice.
It is discouraging that there are only a few
people in jail up to this time; Bernard Madoff
and Frank DiPascali and two computer
programmers. It is beyond believe that they
acted alone. And, I fervently hope that most if
not all Madoff victims live long enough to
receive some reasonable form of restitution
from the resolution of this case. And I hope
that our government takes up the challenge
and fully investigates the complicity of the SEC*

in this unfortunate saga.

When I look in the mirror I see someone who may actually be considered lucky.   Unlike many elderly Madoff victims, I never lived on the Madoff money.   While retirement is now nothing more than an illusion, I do have some years left to work.   I cherish the newfound friends that I have made in the Madoff group although I wish that I had met these wonderful Americans under different circumstances.   And, my family has gotten even closer as we rally around the implications of this government-created disaster.

As I stated earlier, my life is forever changed.

Only <u>one</u> thing remains the same as compared to before December 11, 2008.   I still play tennis at 7 a.m. Sunday through Friday."

The book launch in June of 2010 was quite exciting. Appropriately, it occurred in New York, just outside the Lipstick building where Madoff maintained his offices. The media provided extensive coverage of those appearing for the launch. It served as an opportunity for Madoff victims and fellow book contributors to have a reunion of sorts and engage the press in a discussion of the description of most Madoff investors – distinctly different from that portrayed by the media. One conclusion reached at the luncheon following the launch – we are already old and getting older. Many questioned whether we will live long enough to see the conclusion of the Madoff saga!

Pictures taken in N.Y. at the book launch for "The Club No One Wanted To Join"

Madoff was an equal opportunity criminal

Madoff was an indiscriminate thief – he took money from everyone including union pension plans and charities.

The 29 stories in "The Club No One Wanted to Join" is representative of many individual investors. The organizations discussed below are examples of the many institutions ravaged by Madoff.

The pension plan for Carpenters local 747 in Syracuse, N.Y. had assets of approximately $150 million. About 2/3rds was invested with J.P. Jeanneret Associates, a Madoff feeder fund. Many union members were pensioners receiving monthly payments; much of it funded with profits reported by Jeanneret by Madoff. Pensioners receiving these regular distributions were harmed in two ways – the pension checks stopped immediately – and money received over the past 2 years is potentially subject to litigation by the trustee.

Examples of non-profits invested with Madoff include not only charities with Jewish affiliations but also education and health care institutions. Damaged institutions include the Congregation Kehilath Jeshurun, Gift of Life Bone Marrow Foundation, Hadassah, the Women's Zionist Organization of America, New York Law School, Senator Frank R. Lautenberg's charitable foundation and Tufts University.

Keep in mind that Madoff used his connection to these institutions to enhance his reputation and attract new money.

11 THE VICTIMS ORGANIZE

After the alert on December 11th reporting Madoff was arrested for securities fraud I duped myself into thinking (and hoping) "it happened to the other guy."   I naively deluded myself into believing the existence of the physical brokerage statements BLMIS produced for over 20 years simply could not be faked.   It seemed inconceivable federal regulators at the SEC could utterly fail to discover that such a long running operation of immense magnitude was a fraud.   After all, Madoff promoted successfully passing multiple SEC investigations as a reason to trust the firm. And so, for the next 3 days, I misled myself into thinking those who had invested through less transparent and more loosely regulated mutual funds were the ones who were defrauded.

Wrong!

The arrest of Madoff shook the financial world.   One of their own – and a very big fish – was a crook.   The press discovered some newsworthy event every few hours and the financial news networks covered the event continuously.   By December 14th the press reported that Madoff fooled regulators at the SEC, duped the financial industry, and cheated ALL of his victims (actually almost all since my opinion is that those with non-split-strike accounts knew of the fraud and had already profited greatly).   Those with brokerage statements were not safe!   This buzz saw was going to annihilate both brokerage and feeder fund investors.

The scope of the crime was absolutely breathtaking; tens of thousands of investors; $65 billion in losses.   Surely the authorities would quickly come to the rescue and do their very best to recover what remained for investors.

Mailings from Federal authorities arrived within the first few weeks.   These papers acknowledged that I had an account with BLMIS and my claim was being evaluated.   Sometime before the end of January of 2009 I was interviewed by representatives from the U.S. Attorney's office and the FBI.   Just a few weeks had passed; perhaps this nightmare would end quickly! Aggressive initial activity indicated the wheels of justice were beginning to turn.   Almost four years later they are still turning – very, very slowly!

So what happens when you are the victim of a financial crime in an industry regulated by a Federal agency?   Who takes charge to recover remaining assets?   How are those assets distributed? Do you need a lawyer, and if so, where is the money for legal representation going to come from?   How do you acquire information?   There are other victims; thousands of them. They are my shipmates, sharing a seat in the same leaky boat!   What are they doing?   Is there some way to contact these other victims so we can communicate, share information and perhaps plan a strategy to deal with the agencies that were truly controlling events and making the rules?

Connecting with other victims: Madoff Survivors

On January 23rd, 2009 an article in the Philadelphia Inquirer told a story about a Maureen Ebel who was living in Florida with a Madoff account value of $7.3 million. The story title "She had it made, now she's maid" provided information about a woman who recently entrusted her life savings with Madoff, planned a Florida retirement and now had to return to work as a maid. This was my first opportunity to discuss the fallout from the scandal directly with another investor. I called her at home. Maureen proved to be a delightful person who had contacts with other victims. She led me to Ronnie Sue Ambrosino, who, together with her husband, was reaching out to Madoff victims throughout the country. Ronnie Sue participated in forming a group named "Madoff Survivors." This organization existed for the sole purpose of linking victims together using a secure email conduit to share information. Email communication was a necessity since members were scattered all over the country making it difficult to organize and arrange face-to-face meetings.

Madoff Survivors is a "members only" group for the poor souls who unfortunately invested with Bernard Madoff. On February 3, 2009 I received the following email asking for confirmation that I had indeed invested with Madoff. There was a reason for asking for this assurance. The U.S. Attorney published 163 pages listing names and addresses of Madoff investors – including mine. The news media was using this list to inundate victims with phone interview requests. The press was also trying to gain access to "Madoff survivors" emails meant only for the eyes of involved investors. Thus a concerted effort to validate "members only" to ensure this privileged information would be limited to victims; no press, no attorneys.

> *"Thank you for writing about our group. In*
> *order to ensure that the group consists only of*

former Madoff investors, I'll need to ask a few questions regarding your trade confirmations. There are 3 lines of headings on the form. Please give me the headings in the first line of the form. For instance, the first heading is ORIGINATOR NO. Once you give me these headings, we'll send you an invitation to join Madoff Survivors' Group. We are a group that shares knowledge and offers support to all investors who were defrauded by Bernard Madoff. Please feel free to read all previous postings and to contribute your thoughts and questions. Thank you, we look forward to having you join our group. Until then, Keep The Faith"

Madoff Survivors has approximately 450 members - not very many considering the enormous number of investors, but a very active group. Individually no one knew very much, but by pooling information, members were able to get a much better idea of "next steps." The existence of the group also afforded an opportunity to plan events that might be helpful to the cause. Sometimes these "next steps" meant a rally in N.Y. when Madoff was sentenced; other times it included a planned letter writing "assault" on Congress seeking legislative relief.

This group provided access to a wealth of new information. Members encompassed a wide diversity of professions including CPA's, businessmen, teachers, attorneys and academics. This broad based group allowed input from a variety of perspectives and provided professional opinions about topics of interest to members.

Without "Madoff Survivors" much of the information presented in Volume II of this book series would not be possible.

A page from the 5th lecture of the class shows a few of the tasks undertaken by Madoff Survivors. Via email, members were able to accomplish much, including those tasks listed below.

1. Able to organize a rally in N.Y. for June 29th, 2009 when Madoff was sentenced
2. Organized several letter writing campaigns to members of Congress
3. Find members willing to tell their story in "The Club No One Wanted to Join"
4. Provide assistance for filing tax refunds and reclaiming medicare Part B fees
5. Provide talking points for members willing to speak to the media

The victims groups

- ☐ Who are the members
  - ■ Anyone who invested with Madoff either directly or indirectly through feeder funds
  - ■ Proof of investment required (to exclude press and attorneys)
- ☐ Purpose of the groups
  - ■ Members only email service to
    - ☐ Share information
      - ■ Ask questions of others
      - ■ Provide information to others
    - ☐ Solicit members who are willing to talk to the press
      - ■ Offer talking points for press interviews
    - ☐ Organize letter writing campaign to Judge Dennis Chin who will sentence Bernard Madoff
    - ☐ Organize multiple congressional letter writing campaigns
    - ☐ Organize members when events occur
  - ■ Public Websites
    - ☐ Provide information and guidance about legislation and litigation
    - ☐ Serve as a conduit to share media reports

Only registered and verified victims could access this "members only" means of communicating through "Madoff Survivors." But there was another need. In order to garner widespread support we needed some means of communicating and sharing information with the general public.   The media was always there for a "news worthy" event, but press interest was in ratings; ours was education. "Madoff-help.com" is an extremely detailed website serving as an information source to the general public.   Since this site contains "breaking news" I often display the home page during the course.   Two pages from the course are shown below.   Consider investing a few minutes to look at the current information on this website.

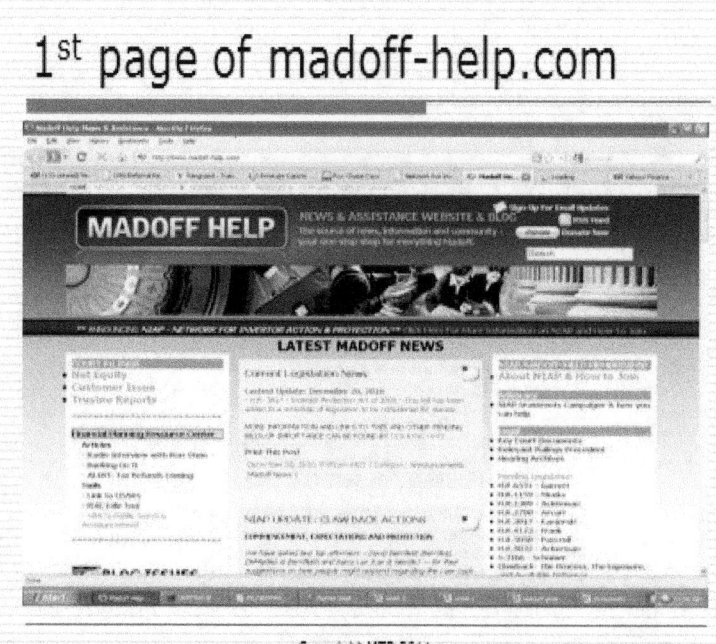

2nd page of madoff-help.com

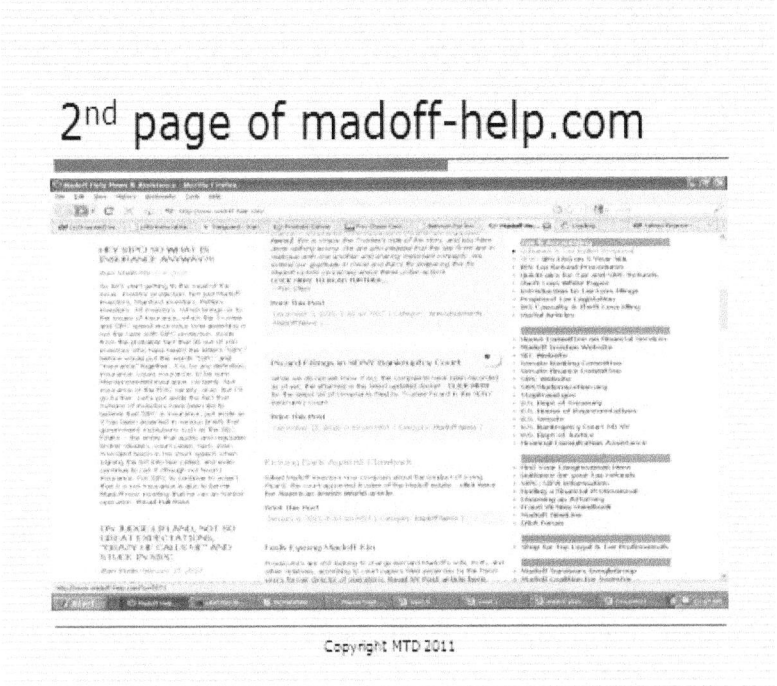

Copyright MTD 2011

Madoff Survivor activity throughout 2009 was enormous; most members spent several hours each day processing 150+ emails. Everyone seemed to have a little piece of data that, once connected, began to paint a picture of the daunting task we all faced. Recovery would be difficult, and it would be slow.

The year is now 4 A.M. (four years After Madoff). There is little "new" information to be discovered. Members of the group are fatigued and disillusioned as they observe painfully slow progress by the trustee and no effective Congressional support. By early 2012 weekly email activity dropped to fewer than 20. It is still declining. Only two emails were circulated in October. I believe the significant drop in activity is not due to apathy – but to resignation! Resignation that Madoff victims are largely on their own. Resignation that Wall Street has won and will never change. Resignation that other investors have no more protection today than we did four years ago.

12 SHOULD INVESTORS HAVE KNOWN MADOFF WAS "TOO GOOD TO BE TRUE"

To succeed, and stay out of jail, Madoff had to dupe investors. He had to convince them he had the best trading system on Wall Street and the returns were real. The trading system he promoted to most clients was the "Split Strike Conversion Strategy." The returns were in a range that investors would find plausible and similar to those reported by other trading operations.

Much has been said in the press about the "unbelievably" high returns generated by Madoff. In order to understand if this argument is valid I went to the financial archives to compare Madoff's IA return to those generated by large mutual funds and by the overall stock market.

Four large mutual fund companies were included in this comparison: American, Fidelity, Janus and Vanguard. These mutual fund companies have many funds covering a range of investing philosophies ranging from S&P index funds to specialty funds such as gold. Since Madoff supposedly invested only in blue chip stocks I selected funds with a long term track record that invested in large cap stocks. This data for the following four charts was reported on Vanguard.com in November of 2009. My personal IA return over the 18 years of my investment horizon was 10.5%, in line with that reported during my discussions with other Madoff investors. I rounded Madoff's return to 11%.

Let's compare four American Funds to BLMIS. All four funds have a track record measured in decades to ensure that the average lifetime annual return is stable. All four funds invest primarily in large cap stocks. All four funds performed BETTER than my BLMIS IA account.

Fund Name	Starting date for the fund	Average lifetime annual return
Growth Fund of America	1978	17.79%
Fundamental	1978	12.03%
Investment Company of America	1934	12.0%
American Mutual	1950	11.4%
Madoff IA investors	~1970	11%

Michael T. De Vita

An analysis of Fidelity, Janus, and Vanguard show a similar pattern. Fourteen of sixteen mutual funds in the comparison set outperformed the BLMIS return. So, why go with Madoff? Why not just select one of these other, better performing competitors? The answer lies with the second promise of Madoff – consistency! The chart shows the annual market returns for 30 years. While the average return for each decade far exceeds that reported by Madoff, the yearly volatility would be frightening to Madoff's conservative investors.

Historical S&P 500 Index Stock Market Returns					
Year	Return	Year	Return	Year	Return
1980	32.40%	1990	-3.20%	2000	-9.10%
1981	-4.90%	1991	30.50%	2001	-11.90%
1982	21.40%	1992	7.70%	2002	-22.10%
1983	22.5	1993	10.00%	2003	28.70%
1984	6.30%	1994	1.30%	2004	10.90%
1985	32.20%	1995	37.40%	2005	4.90%
1986	18.50%	1996	23.10%	2006	15.90%
1987	5.20%	1997	33.40%	2007	5.50%
1988	16.80%	1998	28.60%	2008	-37.00%
1989	31.50%	1999	21.00%	2009	26.50%
Avg	24.1%		19.0%		12.3%

Note that the average for each decade declines from 24% for the 80's to 19% for the 90's and 12% for the next decade. While Madoff underperformed each of these averages, he did produce much more consistent returns for his investors – just as

204

promised.

Contributing to the commonly accepted and correspondingly negative stereotype is the widespread belief that the Madoff investor just had to know the returns were not possible.

I again point to a chapter which I wrote for "The Club No One Wanted to Join" as evidence that Madoff average returns were NOT extraordinary. Indeed the data I uncovered actually proves the opposite - Madoff actually underperformed many large, well known mutual funds.

"SHOULD THE MADOFF RATE OF RETURN HAVE MADE INVESTORS SUSPICIOUS

Who is to blame for the Madoff fraud? Is it the SEC for failing to discover the Ponzi scheme despite repeated investigations? How about the IRS for approving Madoff to handle IRA and pension money? Could it be the employees of Madoff's firm who were exposed to the daily activities of the fraud and yet claim to be totally surprised? Perhaps it was the feeder fund managers who collected large fees while failing to oversee Bernard Madoff's investments. Or is it the individual investors who accepted Madoff as an investment manager for many years?

Most likely, all bear some varying degree of responsibility. Since this book focuses on the individual stories of a number of Madoff investors, this chapter will address the issue of investor responsibility for judging the reasonableness of the returns on their investment accounts.

Madoff investors have been criticized for accepting returns that were reported in the press as being well above those that the average investor would expect to receive by investing in the stock market.

Indeed, a "blame the victim" mentality has been pervasive in the press and many have commented that Madoff investors should have known that the returns reported on their accounts were "too good to be true."

As has been reported by Irving Picard (the trustee handling the bankruptcy) there were two classes of Madoff accounts. Out of almost 5,000 active Madoff accounts there were 245 special accounts that belonged to family members and special friends such as Stanley Chais, Jeffry Picower and others that had a long-standing relationship with Madoff. These special accounts received return rates that were far in excess of those that were reported for the majority of Madoff investors.

Many Madoff investors report that the average return to those 4,755 "non-special" accounts was about 10% to 11% per annum. A number of investors stated that it was not the rate of return that attracted them to invest with Madoff, but rather Madoff's statement that his split-strike conversion strategy generated consistency and predictability with neither large gains nor large losses. While the market can generate large single year gains (the S&P increased 23.5% in 2009 and the NASDAQ increased 44%) Madoff investors would never see such large gains nor would their accounts suffer large losses.

Is an 11% annual return unreasonable?

In order to address the reasonableness of an 11% annual return it is necessary to compare this to the returns an investor would receive from large mutual fund companies that invest in stocks. Four large mutual fund companies that have individual funds with long term track records were selected as the basis for comparison. The four fund companies include: The American Mutual Fund Company, Fidelity Mutual Funds, Janus Mutual Funds and Vanguard Mutual funds. Within each mutual fund company four individual mutual funds were evaluated. Since

Madoff perpetrated his fraud over decades, only funds that have been in business for an extended period were selected. The returns for the selected mutual funds were reported on the Vanguard.com web site in November of 2009.

<u>*Madoff Returns versus American Mutual Fund Company*</u>

Four American Funds were selected for comparison. These four funds were started from 1934 to 1978 and include Growth Fund of America (1978), Fundamental (1978), Investment Company of American (1934) and American Mutual (1950). The chart below shows the average annual return reported by Madoff was actually lower than that for all four American Funds. With the exception of the Growth Fund of American, Madoff's return was within one percentage point of the other three funds.

American Mutual Funds
Average Annual Return

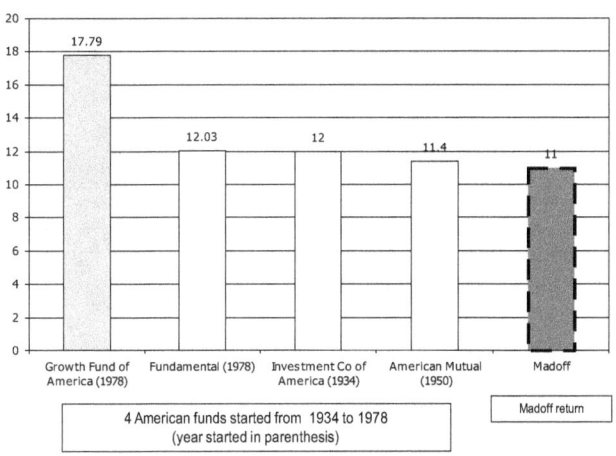

207

Madoff Returns versus Fidelity Mutual Funds

Four Fidelity Funds were selected for comparison. These four funds were started from 1963 to 1985 and include Magellan (1963), Advisor Diversified Stock (1970), Growth (1983) and Advisor Capital Development (1985). The same pattern as observed for American Funds appears for the Fidelity comparison. Madoff's reported annual return was lower than any of these four long-term funds. Again, Madoff's return was within one and a half percentage points of three of the funds. Magellan fund greatly outperformed all three Fidelity funds as well as Madoff.

Fidelity Mutual Funds
Average Annual Return

Returns reported on Vanguard.com website, November 2009

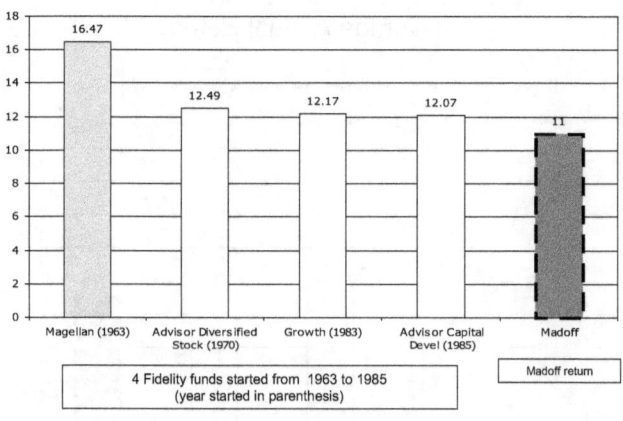

4 Fidelity funds started from 1963 to 1985
(year started in parenthesis)

Madoff return

Madoff Returns versus Janus Mutual Funds

*Four Janus Funds were selected for comparison.   These four
funds were started from 1970 to 1998 and include Small Cap
Value (1987), Mid Cap Value (1998), Janus Fund (1970) and Janus
Twenty (1985).   The annual returns for all four Janus funds were
similar (within 2% points) and all four were greater than that
reported to Madoff investors.*

Janus Mutual Funds
Average Annual Return

Returns reported on Vanguard.com website, November 2009

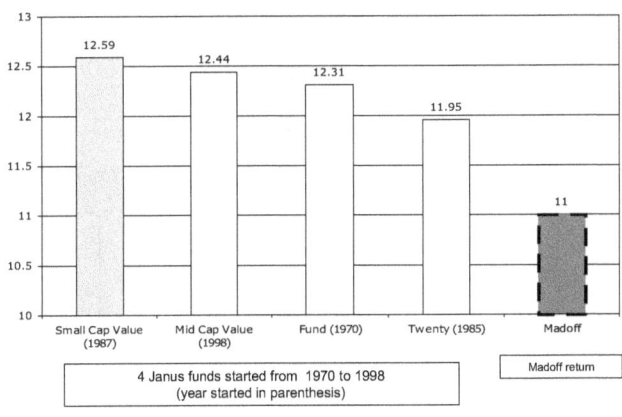

4 Janus funds started from 1970 to 1998
(year started in parenthesis)

Madoff return

Madoff Returns versus Vanguard Mutual Funds

Four Vanguard Funds were selected for comparison. These four funds were started from 1958 to 1984 and include Prime Cap (1984), Windsor (1958), Wellesley Income (1970) and 500 Index (1976). The Vanguard 500 Index was deliberately selected since, as an unmanaged index, it is a surrogate for the average long-term return one might expect by investing in the market. The annual returns for all four Vanguard funds were similar (with 3% points) and only the 500 Index and Wellesley Income returned less than that reported to Madoff investors.

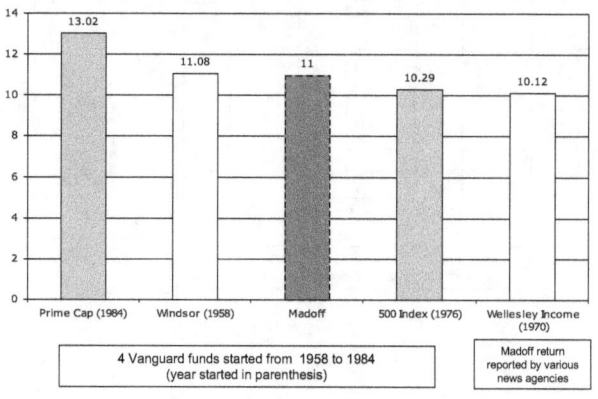

Vanguard Mutual Funds
Average Annual Return

Returns reported on Vanguard.com website, November 2009

Prime Cap (1984) 13.02 · Windsor (1958) 11.08 · Madoff 11 · 500 Index (1976) 10.29 · Wellesley Income (1970) 10.12

4 Vanguard funds started from 1958 to 1984 (year started in parenthesis)

Madoff return reported by various news agencies

Summary: Is an 11% annual return unreasonable?

The above charts demonstrate that returns reported by Madoff for the majority of his investor accounts (not including the 244 "special" accounts) were in line with those that could have been received by depositing that money with four large mutual fund companies and allowing those investments to grow over time. Indeed, Vanguard Index 500 and Wellesley Income are the only funds that performed at a lower level than that reported to Madoff investors for their accounts, and that was by less than 1 percentage point.

Therefore, the returns reported by Madoff were in line with those that an investor might reasonably expect by investing in the market for the long term. Indeed, Madoff likely deliberately reported such a comparable level of return so as not to alarm investors with unreasonably high returns that might raise questions amongst his investors.

Why did they invest with Madoff? Not because of the high rate of return, but because of the safety and predictability promised by his "advanced trading strategy."

Should Madoff investors have been suspicious about the trading in their accounts?

All Madoff direct investors received transactions confirmations whenever Madoff executed trades and received monthly account statements. These statements showed stock and Treasury Bill transactions for large cap stocks that actually traded on the exchange.

The individual investor would not be alarmed by the rate of return, nor by the types of trades that were supposedly executed. The individual investor would not have the power or authority to go to Madoff's office and examine his books to determine if those

trades actually occurred.   Only the SEC had that power – and
they failed to use it appropriately leading to the largest Ponzi
scheme crime in the history of the nation and the world."

13 MOVING ON

<u>My personal efforts to inform and educate</u>

You have a right to know the details of what really happened, not just relative to Madoff but also to his investors.

You will not get this from the press, from our government or from any of the various books written about the topic. The time and effort to collect, synthesize, organize and report the material for my course which was used to create this book is too valuable to present to the limited audiences I can personally reach.

I have made a concerted effort to collect and distribute information about the Madoff scandal. This effort includes a willingness to give presentations to virtually any group asking for them. Another slide from my class shows the various personal appearances I have made thus far.

Where I have spoken/appeared

- ☐ May 12, 2009: Radio show for Morning Call
- ☐ June 2, 2009: Pa. Professional House Licensure Committee (Harrisburg, Pa.)
- ☐ June 29, 2009: NYC Federal Court
- ☐ December 2, 2009: Washington D.C. congressional hearing
- ☐ December 2009 issue of Philadelphia Magazine: "Uncle Sham"
- ☐ August 26, 2010: Community Meeting, Montgomery County
- ☐ June 2010: Co-author of the book "The Club No One Wanted To Join"
- ☐ September 23, 2010: Washington D.C. congressional hearing
- ☐ October 5, 2010: "Meet The Author", DelVal College
- ☐ November 15, 2010: Blue Bell Country Club Women's Group
- ☐ February through April, 2011: Class at DelVal CLR Program "Can You Sleep At Night"
- ☐ April 7, 2011: Radio appearance for "The Story"
- ☐ May 13, 2011: Washington D.C. congressional hearing
- ☐ April 20, 2011: Kiwanis Club of Doylestown
- ☐ October 2011: Class at DelVal CLR Program
- ☐ April 20, 2012: Temple University School of Business
- ☐ Multiple Newspaper articles and TV appearances

Speaking to a variety of groups as well as to multiple media outlets resulted in some unexpected questions and events.

The Temple University talk with undergraduates was quite interesting. It was my first, and thus far only, opportunity to talk to young people. This presented some unusual questions such as a more detailed explanation of a 1099 (one student said – we spend money not make it, at least not yet). It turned out that several of the students were working on advanced degrees and I suggested that one of them might want to contact me regarding a topic for a possible thesis or dissertation. The class material presented a wealth of information which could be used for several topics including business ethics on Wall Street, governmental supervision of the brokerage industry, investor protection afforded by mandated industry insurance programs or perhaps a paper on the effect of brokerage fraud on investor confidence in the financial system.

Prior to the June 2009 Madoff sentencing hearing I placed a call to the White House asking to speak with the President about an urgent matter. Needless to say – I did not get very far. After being transferred to the White House Comment Line I found that actually speaking with a senior politician was not possible. I was told that no one paid much attention to the Comment Line for weeks or months. Any significant reaction was dependent on the number of incoming calls on a specific topic and I could be quite sure that the Madoff topic was not popular on the Line. It was clear that I needed to bypass the Comment Line and speak with a real person. I called again telling the operator "I was calling on behalf of the Wall Street Journal and would like to speak with the person in the White House Press office detailed to respond to questions on the Madoff scandal." While this was not an outright untruth, it did stretch the facts quite a bit. I never said I "worked for" the Journal, merely that I was calling on "behalf of" – I figured that since my picture and comments were in the Journal the past few days I could justify the slight exaggeration. I found that there was no specific person assigned to answer questions on this topic.

One reporter who came to the house asked if I had really called the White House. After an affirmative response, she asked if I could call again so they could record the call. This call yielded something different than a perfunctory transfer to the Comment Line. I was told that the President was out of the country and was not available for a discussion. In jest (after all, I was asking for the impossible) I asked if I could arrange a lunch or coffee when he returned. When that too was denied because "he was very busy" I went down the entire cabinet asking to speak with each one of them. Not surprisingly, each request was denied.

Below are some pictures which were taken at various events.

Rep. Mike Fitzpatrick (Pa. 8th congressional district) – guest speaker at Fall 2011 class

Congressional hearing in Washington, D.C., Mike Fitzpatrick as co-chairman

Representative Patrick Murphy news conference in late 2009

Radio talk show "The Story"

Temple University talk to undergraduates

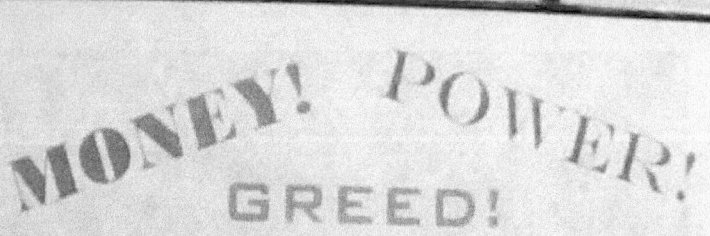

MONEY! POWER!
GREED!

**Bernie Madoff, The SEC, SIPC,
And The Decline Of Trust
In The U.S. Securities Industry**

The Office of Distance Learning and Summer Programs
invites you to attend this Information Session

Date: Wednesday, April 25th
Time: 3:00 p.m. to 4:00 p.m.
Location: Tuttleman 103

Bernard Madoff committed the largest financial crime in the
history of the Country. $65 billion of client money
disappeared on December 11, 2008 leaving tens of thousands of
his investors to deal with a myriad of financial, legal and moral
issues that will last for years.

Michael Devita is a 20-year Madoff investor with firsthand
experience with the Madoff fraud. The information for this lecture
was gleaned from over 4,000 pages of litigation filed by the trustee
liquidating the Madoff business and personal empires.

R.S.V.P. by Friday, April 20th
email: online@temple.edu
or call (215) 204-2712

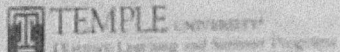
TEMPLE UNIVERSITY

Poster advertising the talk at Temple University

The second book of this series will help you to understand the role of the SEC (Securities Exchange Commission) in failing to discover the crime and the impact of the event on Madoff's victims today, and on you tomorrow.

As the final words in this book I point you to a Congressional hearing in Washington D.C. on February 4th, 2009 when Representative Gary Ackerman (N.Y. 5th congressional district) questioned members of the SEC about the agency's role in the financial mess created by Madoff.

(Rep. Ackerman) *I am frustrated beyond belief. We are talking to ourselves and you are pretending to be here. I really do not understand what is going on. The previous witness said that you guys as an agency act like you are deaf, dumb and blind. Now I figure that you by coming here you were going to testify in front of Congress. And don't dare tell anyone you testified in front of Congress. You are going to be subject to a violation of false advertising laws. You told us nothing. And I believe that is your intention. I figured you would leave your blindfold, and your duct tape and your earplugs behind, but you seem to be wearing them today. Instead of telling us anything you read from the*

preamble of your mission statement and you broke it up into five segments.

What the heck went on! Your mission, you said was to "protect investors and detect fraud quickly." How did that work out? What went wrong? It seems to me a private, with all of your investigators and all of your agency that you all described, one guy, with a few friends and helpers discovered this thing nearly a decade ago, led you to this pile of dung that is Bernie Madoff and stuck your nose in it. And you couldn't figure it out! You could not find your backside with two hands if the lights were on. Can you explain yourselves?

You have single handedly diffused the American public of any sense of confidence in our financial markets if you are the watchdogs. You have totally and thoroughly failed in your mission. Don't you get it?

And now, other people are investigating what you should have found out. And you are hiding behind "well maybe we can't talk because someone else is looking at it." Well, you forfeited your right to investigate by not doing it. Certainly not doing it properly or adequately. And now you are telling us that because other people are looking at it you are not going to tell us what is going on. Like hell you won't! What happened here? (long pause) That is a question.

Do we start with hear no evil, see no evil or do no evil? Take your pick

(long pause as he stares at the table of SEC employees) I only have 5 minutes. Someone has to start.

(Linda Thompson, SEC Enforcement Director) Let me start with enforcement. As I said, we did an investigation, an investigation in 2006 and it was closed without action.

(Rep. Ackerman) Why was it closed without action? What did you investigate. What methodology did you use?

(Thompson) And if you, if you let me introduce.

(Rep. Ackerman) Was it suspicious that a one man accounting firm investigating a $50 billion dollar empire? And you keep saying "alleged, alleged." This guy confessed on national TV you might have noticed.

(Thompson) Our objective is to actually hold him accountable in a court of law bearing in mind (interrupted)

(Rep. Ackerman) You missed your chance.

(Thompson) We have a pending action in the Southern District of N.Y.

(Rep. Ackerman) You took your action after the guy confessed. Don't give yourself any pat on the back for that.

(Thompson) Congressman, every time (interrupted)

(Rep. Ackerman) Why didn't you find him is the question?

(Thompson) I understand your question. And we cannot answer as to the specifics. I can talk generally (interrupted)

(Rep. Ackerman) You know if anybody made the case better than Mr. Markopolis, and I did not think that anybody could, that you people being completely inept. You made the case better than him.

(Thompson) Well sir, I am sorry that you feel that way. Personally (interrupted)

(Rep. Ackerman) I think I am reflecting what the American public feels. How are they supposed to have confidence that if someone does go to you with a complaint, gives it to you on a silver platter. With all of the investigation with all of the numbers, all of the data, telling you exactly what he did, how he did it and how he knows that. And after a period of a half a dozen or eight years – you don't know anything.

(Thompson) I can only talk about what we do overall.

(Rep. Ackerman) No, no. We want to know specifically. I do not care about what your general purpose in life is. I don't need you to come here and tell me that you hate fraud. I hate when that happens, don't you. You are supposed to find it out before it happens.

(Thompson) In enforcement obviously we can't. And I understand that concern. In enforcement we bring – last year we brought six hundred and seventy some odd cases. In the past two years we brought 70 cases involving Ponzi schemes. In those 70 cases (interrupted)

(Rep. Ackerman) Listen. Listen. I am sure you have medals and ribbons and stuff like that. Congratulations on all the good stuff you have done. I don't want to belittle any of that. But this is huge. How do you miss that! And, we know that there are mini Madoffs' out there. They are starting to surface. You missed all of those too! This one you were pointed at. And, Mr. Markopolis says he is going to give you another one tomorrow. But he is going to give it to someone else because nobody has any confidence in you guys anymore.

Most of us speak English, and we're having a hard time understanding you.

Your value to the American people is worthless. Your contribution to this proceeding is zero.

Our economy is in crisis. **We thought the enemy was Mr. Madoff. I think it's you.**

In Volume II we will focus on the following topics.

1. Details of the multiple SEC investigations of Madoff; what they knew, when they knew it, and what they did with the information available to them.

2. How investors approached Congress to seek the assistance of legislators.

3. Specific laws that were proposed to assist all brokerage Ponzi scheme victims; and which ones were passed.

4. The role of the SIPC trustee in determining which investors are covered by SIPC, which ones are not, and what government can do to ensure that your brokerage statement carries legal weight.

5. Details of what whistleblowers told regulators about Madoff and what regulators did with that information.

6. Details of other financial crimes including Alan Stanford of Stanford International, and Jon Corzine of MF Global.

7. Suggestions for how you can avoid a similar fate. Remember that this is not just a book about the past of Bernard Madoff and his victims. It is also a story about the future – perhaps your future if you believe in the believability of your brokerage account.

Stay tuned.

www.ingramcontent.com/pod-product-compliance
Lightning Source LLC
Chambersburg PA
CBHW071414170526
45165CB00001B/270